PREACHING
ROMANS

Preaching Classic Texts

PREACHING
ROMANS

BRUCE E.
SHIELDS

CHALICE
PRESS
ST. LOUIS, MISSOURI

Cover art: Tapestry of Saint Paul preaching in Athens by Raphael. Pinacoteca, Vatican Museums. Photo: Scala/Art Resource, NY
Cover design: Michael Foley/Elizabeth Wright
Interior design: Wynn Younker
Art Director: Michael Domínguez

This book is printed on acid-free, recycled paper.

Visit Chalice Press on the World Wide Web at
www.chalicepress.com

10 9 8 7 6 5 4 3 2 1   04 05 06 07 08 09

Library of Congress Cataloging–in–Publication Data

Shields, Bruce.
  Preaching Romans / Bruce Shields.
    p. cm. – (Preaching classic texts)
  ISBN 0-827229-79-8 (pbk. : alk. paper)
  ISBN 978-0-827229-79-8
  1. Bible. N.T. Romans–Homiletical use. I. Title. II. Series.
  BS2665.54.S54 2004
  227'.106–dc22   2004011556

Dedication

The faithful preachers I have known from my childhood to the present have continually renewed my zeal for the proclamation of the evangel in ways both biblical and inventive. I dedicate this book to the memory of two of them who are gone from this life and whose names are recognized in too small a circle: Lee Robinson and Burton Doyle. God grant that their numbers increase.

Contents

It seems I have been preparing for thirty years to write this book. During my eighteen years of steady preaching, I was constantly called back to the writing and preaching of Paul and especially to Romans. My dissertation (*Creation in Romans*) began in a study of Paul's sermon in Athens (Acts 17), from which I was led to study how Paul used themes of creation in this epistle. My teaching since the completion of the dissertation (1980) has been evenly divided between studies of Paul's writings and preaching.

I have lectured on preaching from Romans at Springdale College in Selly Oak, Birmingham, England, and at the Westwood Christian Foundation in Los Angeles. I have taught courses on Romans and preaching from Romans for Emmanuel School of Religion, where I continue to teach. I have led local congregational Bible studies through the book, thus getting feedback from "normal" people. Recently, I published an essay in a *Festschrift*[1] on the subject. I offer this fuller analysis to help preachers better to reflect the concern of the apostle for the proclamation of the gospel.

The Nature of the Book

This book does not masquerade as a complete treatment of anything in Romans. The lists of further reading included at the close of the chapters in part 1 and the bibliography at the end of the Introduction are testimony to other works that treat more fully the texts and topics I only summarize here. I have written these chapters with the busy preacher in mind. I have been in your shoes, so I know the challenges of your vocation. In some instances, you will want to study further after reading a chapter, but in most cases you will not have time to do that. Therefore, I have cut to the central issues and aspects of the texts to help you develop the sermons your congregation needs to hear to understand, appreciate, and commit themselves to the gospel for which Paul gave his life.

Except where I have done some of my own translating or referred to other versions, the biblical texts quoted are from the *New Revised Standard Version Bible.*[2]

I offer the sermons in part 2 to illustrate how we can preach from Romans. They are not intended to be applied to every preaching situation. You who preach are welcome to use ideas and structures you find there, but I trust you to state and illustrate the ideas and to customize the structures to fit your preaching situation. My prayer is that the book will enrich the life of the church and expand the influence of the Lord through the ministry of each reader.

Acknowledgments

I owe a debt of gratitude to many people for enriching my understanding of Paul and his epistle. Professor Peter Stuhlmacher, my *Doktorvater,* pushed me toward many insights and directly pointed out many others to me. My many students over the years have shown interest and asked questions that continue to motivate my own study. My colleagues at Lincoln Christian Seminary and Emmanuel School of Religion have encouraged me more than they can know. Sunday School classes at Grandview Christian Church and First Christian Church, both of Johnson City and the Imitators of Christ men's group at the Hopwood Memorial Christian Church, have helped me by hearing and responding to many of the ideas in the book. My family, who at times I am sure got tired of my excited conversation about the meaning of Greek words in Romans, have supported me in spite of everything. Jon Berquist, Trent Butler, and others of the staff of Chalice Press have helped and encouraged me greatly.

General Approach to the Epistle

A writer dealing with Romans faces a great challenge: most of the book is controversial in one way or another. Scholars argue interminably about exegetical details and major issues. The exception to this is the integrity of the text itself. The only recent scholar to offer serious objections to the authorship of Paul of all sixteen chapters of the epistle is J. C. O'Neill in his Penguin commentary.[1] Otherwise, the world of Pauline scholarship agrees that Paul wrote (or rather dictated) the epistle to the Christians in Rome around 56 C.E. and that all sixteen chapters belonged to the original.

Beyond that agreement lies the land of scholarly controversy. The letter is the longest of Paul's canonical writings and originated relatively late in the apostle's life. Its content is packed with mature thought about the primary issues of Christian faith and about the nature of faith itself. That would be enough reason to keep students of the text busy thinking, but big questions also abound about the historical situation that called for the writing in the first place.

Whereas Galatians and 2 Corinthians are openly polemical and include clear information about opponents of Paul in those communities, the polemic of Romans is more subtle. Here Paul is more guarded in what he says about opponents. He mentions, for instance, in chapter 3 that some are accusing him of preaching a cheap grace message, but even there he does not make it clear that those accusers are in Rome or that he assumes their accusation has reached Rome.

Scholars have lined up on both sides of this question. Many follow the lead of F. C. Baur and his Tübingen school of the early nineteenth century in identifying the controversy between Jewish and Gentile Christian missions as the primary (almost exclusive) stress point of the early church. The scholars on that side assume that the so-called Judaizers, described clearly in Galatians, must have dogged Paul's tracks everywhere he went and that their accusations must have reached Rome before he was able to visit there.

Others, however, are more cautious about this assumption. Mark Nanos[2] argues that Rome and Galatia should be kept separate. He sees Paul in Romans urging the Christians (recently arrived back in Rome after having been expelled by Emperor Claudius) to live in peace with the Jews in Rome, including those who were resisting faith in the Christ. He points out that the instructions Paul gave in Romans 14–15 about living in toleration of differing opinions reflects the instruction given in the apostolic letter sent from the Jerusalem conference to the Gentile churches (Acts 15).

Since Paul mentioned several purposes for his letter, wide room stands open for argument on the matter of the purpose and occasion. Many doctrinal issues continue to be contested: the nature of faith, the meaning of righteousness and of justification, the extent of divine revelation, the ultimate destiny of Israel, the relationship of law and gospel, the place of the Hebrew Scriptures among Christians. These and other topics will remain controversial for the foreseeable future.

This does not mean, however, that preachers must wait for scholars to come to a consensus before preaching on these texts or these topics. Quite the contrary, I would contend that preachers should have a strong voice in the process of coming to an understanding of Paul for our day. As preachers, we have the responsibility (and in Paul's view, the grace and privilege) to return the thoughts of the apostle to their original form— spoken word.

One problem of biblical scholarship since the Reformation is that it has dealt with texts as though inkmarks on a page were the primary means of communication. The words we read were originally spoken: stories were told, sermons and prophecies were preached, psalms and prayers were recited, proverbs were taught, and even the letters were dictated. In Romans, we have the rare privilege of knowing the name of the scribe who took down Paul's spoken words. He identifies himself in 16:22 as "Tertius, the writer of this letter."

So when we accept the task of preaching from Romans, we are taking the written forms of Tertius (and scribes and translators since) and turning them back into spoken forms, as Paul originated them. We need not be bothered that we speak a different language than Paul. He spoke several different languages himself (Acts 21:37–22:2), so his message was not dependent on a specific language. We can be assured that the gospel Paul preached and that Tertius, his amanuensis, recorded was meant to be passed on in spoken form by believers everywhere. Most students of the literature assume that the letter would have been read aloud in one or more assemblies of believers in Rome. The reader may well have been Phoebe, who apparently carried the letter from Paul in Corinth to the Romans as she went there on business (Rom. 16:1–2).

As we preach, we might even be getting closer to the original intent of the apostle than analytical scholars ever will. We can learn much from the work of analysis, but the purpose of the word is not fulfilled until the people for whom God intended it hear it.

For this reason, the first chapter of this book will deal with Paul's understanding of preaching (and to some extent his practice), as shown primarily in Romans. We shall then proceed to deal with some of the primary issues Paul deals with in the epistle and then a few representative passages in a way that I hope will help preachers find meaty messages in passages we have too little space to deal with.

Exegetical Methods Appropriate to Epistolary Literature

When we begin reading any letter from former times, we become aware we are listening in on somebody else's conversation and are hearing only one side of that exchange.

This presents the interpreter with challenges in the best of circumstances. Even if we are well acquainted with the sender and the receiver(s) of the letter, we still face the need to "read between the lines" if we are to understand everything written. When those involved originally with the letter are removed from us by time, space, culture, and language differences, the challenges become even more daunting. In the case of Romans, we are almost two millennia removed from its origin in about 56 C.E. Most of us live an ocean away from Europe. Twenty-first-century culture differs radically from that of the first-century Roman Empire. Even for the best students of the Bible, koine Greek is at best a second language for us. So to exegete the meaning of the epistle, we must fill those gaps with as much information and empathy as possible, building our understanding of the apostle, of the early church, of the Roman culture, and the Greek language until we begin to feel at home with the letter.

This task is not as formidable as it might seem, since scholars have been amassing such data for several centuries. In fact, the challenge facing the student of the apostle is reading through the mass of information and deciding what is trustworthy and relevant. I write this book to help busy preachers get a grip on such historical information.

To this end I shall be offering readers the background information needed to put a passage in an understandable framework. At times the relevant information will deal with Jewish background materials from the Hebrew Bible and other Jewish writings. For other passages, it will be Hellenistic or Roman cultural or political information, including rhetorical uses. We shall investigate the appearance of certain terms in other Pauline writings, elsewhere in the Bible, and in other relevant literature. In these and other ways, we shall be searching for the meaning of the text in its historical setting.

However, deciding what the text meant does not guarantee we know what the text signifies for us and the hearers of our sermons. We must add some theological reflection and exegesis of our own settings to the "historical-grammatical" exegesis so we can bridge the gap of time and culture between Paul and our pulpits. Even with passages that deal with issues foreign to us, we can find enough theological and anthropological principles at work to apply to situations peculiar to our own time and place.

To get at those principles, we must forego any attempts to read Paul legalistically. This is not a text of rules to be applied in any and every situation. This is a window on how Paul approached an early Christian community with the purpose of developing a good relationship with them and of helping them resolve some relational stress among themselves.

My general understanding of what Paul was doing with the Roman letter is what I call "gospel logic." He wrote the letter as a church-planting missionary who was planning to journey farther west in the Empire than he had gone before. Therefore, he needed the support of the Christians in Rome to undergird his mission to Spain. He was acquainted with several believers in Rome but had never visited there; so, he presented to them the way he preached the gospel to non-believers. He began with the reality and effects of sin in the lives of both Jews and Gentiles and continued through the good news of forgiveness by the grace of God in Christ to the shape of the lives of the redeemed. At that point he turned the light of the gospel on some specific issues in Rome concerning how Christians should live in relation to one another and to the larger community.

How We Might Preach on Romans

Romans has been so thoroughly analyzed and so highly revered down through church history that it may intimidate us. Add to this present-day preachers' preference for narrative texts over the more didactic texts such as Romans, and we preachers face a dilemma. However, this should not deter us. The reason Romans has been so respected and analyzed is that the church has recognized its importance and relevance in every age. Our age is no exception. If we can put the letter in its historical setting, we shall see the narrative's outlines, of which it is but one part: the story of the life and ministry of Paul, as well as the story of the church in Rome.

Romans is a work from which we can lift a passage to deal with a particular issue, or in which we can find texts for a series of issue-related sermons. We might at least once in a ministry preach a course of sermons through the book and communicate the whole gospel message as preached and taught by the apostle to the Gentiles. I would also recommend that a preacher try at least once to preach one sermon on the whole epistle. You might want to use a shorter letter first, but dealing with all sixteen chapters of Romans is possible. To do so you must first decide on a brief passage that you see as a summary of the whole or as the fulcrum of the argument or even as the climax of the presentation of the gospel. Alexander Campbell did this in his "Sermon on the Law,"[3] for which he took Romans 8:3 as the stated text and from there dealt with the meaning and implications of Paul's understanding of the relationship of the Mosaic law to the Christian gospel.

Romans in History

As is true with any text, an understanding of the place Romans occupied in the life of its author and of its recipients can help us to see how it functioned in its original setting. Few scholars doubt that the apostle Paul wrote the epistle pretty much as we have it. Saul of Tarsus claims to have been born into a strict Jewish family and educated as a Pharisee (Phil. 3:5–6). His familiarity with the Hebrew Scriptures becomes obvious as one reads his writings. According to Acts 7 and 8, Saul burst on the scene as a persecutor of the fledgling church, only to be turned around by a vision of Christ while on his way from Jerusalem to arrest Christians in Damascus. This dramatic conversion and call to carry the gospel to the Gentiles changed Saul's life radically.

His first attempts to carry out this new commission seem to have been remarkable only in the dangers they exposed the new convert to. He then returned to his home region in Syria, where fourteen years later (see Gal. 1:18 and 2:1), Barnabas found him and brought him to Antioch to help with the growing community of Christians there. Saul and Barnabas were soon dispatched to preach in Galatia where they had some success. The name *Saul* had during this period been replaced by the more Hellenistic name *Paulos.*

The epistle to the Romans was written during a third mission journey of the apostle, probably 56 or 57 C.E. Paul wrote it from Corinth as he waited for the spring weather to make it possible to sail back to Jerusalem (see Acts 20:2–3). His relationship with the church in Corinth had been rocky, but he had restored a solid relationship with his children in the faith there. Paul's next journey was to be westward to Spain, and he needed a supply center farther west than Antioch, where most of his support had come from. Rome would be ideal, but he had never visited the Christians there. He did, however, have several friends and acquaintances there, so he was encouraged to write to the church in Rome.

Paul wrote this letter at the height of his powers after years of effective mission work in the eastern half of the Roman empire. He had big plans for more work ahead of him, so he took time to think through some issues and write carefully to establish a relationship with the church in Rome. In so doing, he helped the church with some of their internal stresses.

Rome was, of course, the major city of the Mediterranean world of the first and succeeding centuries. It was a city of well over a million people, including the leading purveyors of power and the lowliest of slaves. It included a sizeable Jewish population with a number of synagogues.

The circumstances surrounding the founding of the Christian church in Rome are matters of speculation. Acts makes no mention of it, and most later information is legendary. The one hint Acts gives us is the "visitors from Rome" mentioned among those present at the temple in Jerusalem for the first preaching of the gospel on Pentecost (Acts 2:10–11). For some reason Luke recorded that these Romans included "both Jews and converts to Judaism." It is likely, then, that the gospel was first heard in Rome when these visitors, especially if they were among the 3,000 baptized that day, returned to their homes and synagogues.

This would indicate that the gospel had been working at least among Jews in Rome for at least 24 years. Paul wrote his epistle to a well-established community of Christians. The church had begun without any direct help from an apostle and had continued to see things primarily through the eyes of the Jewish Diaspora community. It appears that they had been quite successful in evangelizing Gentiles, since the stresses Paul dealt with in the later chapters include some misunderstandings between Jews and Gentiles. The recipients of this letter, then, consisted of a mix of Jews and Gentiles, well-established in the Christian faith and quite knowledgeable of the Hebrew Scriptures.

The Form and Purpose of Romans

We shall deal with matters of form as we look at specific texts in the letter. The term *letter* is misleading because the combination of personal letter and essay was common in Paul's day. Philosophers and others conveyed their thinking in this form. Paul started to write a personal letter. As was the custom, he began with his name, the designation of the recipients, a greeting, and a prayer of thanksgiving for the recipients. He closed the letter with personal greetings to individuals and families among the recipients, including greetings from Paul's companions and fellow workers.

Between the opening and closing sections, we have an essay that begins with a discussion of sin and ends with exhortations to specific ways of acting and relating. This is not what we think of as systematic theology although it does appear to have a thought-out form. What I call "gospel logic" appears to have a sermonic form. It begins with a description of the need of people for the grace of God. That is, it begins with the universality of sin. It goes on to describe how God's grace in the crucifixion and resurrection of Jesus Christ makes possible the forgiveness of sin and the power to escape sin's domination. Along the way, Paul dealt with the tangential yet important issue of the place of Judaism in the strategy of God for the salvation of the human race. He concluded, in chapters 12–16, with advice and examples of how a person should live in the light of God's gracious acts of redemption on our behalf.

The big issue that Romans scholars debate is Paul's purpose in writing the epistle. For several centuries, Bible students treated Romans as a "compendium of the Christian religion"[4] or at least as a general survey of the theology of the apostle Paul.[5] But lately, people have begun to make connections between the epistle's content and a likely scenario in the Christian community at Rome.[6]

The author's stated purpose was to win the trust or friendship of the Roman Christians so they would welcome him to Rome and help him on his next missionary thrust westward to Spain (1:10–15; 15:14–33). However, the ethical teaching in chapters 14 and 15 is so specific that it forces the reader to consider a possible application in the Roman church. Chapter 16 shows that Paul had enough acquaintances in Rome that he could have known about serious tensions between Jewish and non-Jewish members there. In addition to his stated purpose, Paul probably intended to help the Roman Christians over this hurdle with which he was already all too familiar.

My working hypothesis is that Paul had these issues in mind as he composed the epistle. A person as complex as Paul probably did not have a single purpose in writing. The first eleven chapters are written as an explication or introduction of the author's understanding of the message he had been preaching all over the eastern regions of the Roman Empire. This would be a sensible way for a missionary to develop a relationship with a prospective supporting church. Since he had not visited Rome before this, he would be aware many people would have little or no information about him or his missionary methods.

At the same time, Paul's close relationship with Priscilla and Aquilla (and apparently other individuals and families in Rome) gave him a source of information about the church in the capital. Paul's pastoral heart and concern for unity among the faithful, as demonstrated in his other letters, must have motivated him to apply the gospel in a way that would be helpful to the recipients. This, of course, would also demonstrate another aspect of Paul's preaching: a specific and concrete local application of the gospel. So, I work with the assumption that Paul's purpose for Romans is connected with his mission westward and the internal unity of the Roman church.

The Place of Romans in Church History

The book of Romans has played a dramatic role in the history of the church. Church history can be seen as a history of the interpretation of the Bible, so the understanding of any Bible book has been from time to time crucial in that history.

But Romans seems to have been involved in nearly every major turning point in the history of the church.

It is impossible to evaluate the total impact the epistle made on the early church, but it was certainly profound. By the end of the first century Romans and other writings of the apostle Paul were being copied and circulated generally among the churches. Around 96 C.E., Clement of Rome quoted Paul's Roman letter as authoritative—most likely quoting from a single copy and not from a collection of Paul's letters. We know that about three years after the writing of the epistle, Paul was welcomed warmly to Rome by the Christians there (Acts 28:14–15). From these bits of information, we can deduce that the book was accepted from the beginning as an important and authoritative document. Within forty years of its writing, Romans was being copied and circulated as Scripture.

This importance has continued for more than 1900 years. The warning of 2 Peter 3:15 is illustrated in the life of a man named Marcion. Around 140 C.E., Marcion listed the New Testament documents he accepted as authoritative. Romans and some other portions of Pauline books were on his list. In fact, Marcion used the Pauline writings he accepted as authentic as the major criterion for judging the other books. Marcion was a Gnostic who tried to separate the gospel from the message of the Hebrew Bible. The Gnostics held that God was a perfect spirit and could have nothing to do with matter. Therefore, Marcion did not want to identify Yahweh, the creator God of the Hebrews, with the Lord God of Jesus. Marcion was eventually disfellowshipped by the Roman church for heresy; his attempt to judge the content of the whole Bible by what he read in Romans and Galatians shows the power of the Roman epistle in the church of the second century.

About 240 years later in Milan, a young man wrestled with God by reading Romans. This man later became a bishop and the most powerful voice of the church of his day and for some time beyond. His name was Augustine. He later described that experience in these words:

> So I was speaking and weeping in the most bitter contrition of my heart, when, lo! I heard from a

neighboring house a voice as of boy or girl, I know not, chanting, and oft repeating, "Take up and read; Take up and read." Instantly, my countenance altered. I began to think most intently whether children were wont in any kind of play to sing such words; nor could I remember ever to have heard the like. So checking the torrent of my tears, I arose; interpreting it to be no other than a command from God to open the book, and read the first chapter I should find.... Eagerly then I returned to the place where Alypius was sitting; for there I had laid the volume of the Apostle when I arose thence. I seized, opened, and in silence read that section on which my eyes first fell: Not in rioting and drunkenness, not in chambering and wantonness, not in strife and envying; but put ye on the Lord Jesus Christ, and make no provision for the flesh, in concupiscence. No further would I read; nor needed I: for instantly at the end of this sentence, by a light as it were of serenity infused into my heart, all the darkness of doubt vanished away.[7]

Then as the dawn was breaking at the close of what we call the Dark Ages, in the spring of 1515, Martin Luther, the young seminary professor, began a series of lectures on Romans. These lectures continued for eighteen months and exerted a powerful influence on his life and on subsequent church history. Here are his comments on the preparation he made for those lectures:

I greatly longed to understand Paul's epistle to the Romans and nothing stood in the way but that one expression, "the justice of God" because I took it to mean that justice whereby God is just and deals justly in punishing the unjust. My situation was that, although an impeccable monk, I stood before God as a sinner troubled in conscience, and I had no confidence that my merit would assuage him. Therefore, I did not love a just and angry God, but rather hated and murmured against him. Yet I clung to the dear Paul and had a great yearning to know what he meant.

Night and day I pondered until I saw the connection between the justice of God and the statement that "the just shall live by his faith." Then, I grasped that the justice of God is that righteousness by which through grace and sheer mercy God justifies us through faith. Thereupon, I felt myself to be reborn and to have gone through the open doors into paradise. The whole of Scripture took on a new meaning, and whereas before the "justice of God" had filled me with hate, now it became to me inexpressibly sweet in greater love. This passage of Paul became to me a gate to heaven.[8]

Later, as Luther prepared to publish his translation of the New Testament, he wrote this paragraph to begin a preface to Romans:

This epistle is in truth the most important document in the New Testament, the whole gospel in its purest expression. Not only is it well worth a Christian's while to know it word for word by heart, but also to meditate on it day by day. It is the soul's daily bread, and can never be read too often or studied too much. The more you probe into it the more precious it becomes, and the better its flavour.[9]

More than two hundred years later, in a small Moravian chapel in Aldersgate Street, London, the words of that preface changed the life of young John Wesley and through him the religious complexion of England and America. It was May 1738. Wesley had spent several years with little success evangelizing the American Indians in Georgia. He returned to England discouraged, conscious that something was lacking. He reported the following:

In the evening, I went very unwillingly to a society in Aldersgate Street, where one was reading Luther's preface to the *Epistle to the Romans.* About a quarter of nine, while he was describing the change which God works in the heart through faith in Christ, I felt my heart strangely warmed. I felt I did trust in Christ, Christ alone for my salvation; and an assurance was given me that he had taken away my sins, even mine, and saved me from the law of sin and of death.[10]

Less than one hundred more years had passed before a young preacher named Alexander Campbell preached a sermon on Romans 8:3 to a meeting of the Redstone Baptist Association at Cross Creek, Virginia, on August 30, 1816. This sermon defined the difference Campbell saw between the authority of the Hebrew Bible and that of the New Testament on the individual Christian and the church. This precipitated a movement of believers on the American continent that, less than two centuries later, has produced thousands of congregations of people known variously as Christian Churches, Churches of Christ, and Disciples of Christ.

The history of the church in the twentieth century continues to be punctuated by contact with Romans. In 1916, when theological liberalism had reached its zenith and World War I shocked Europe, Karl Barth published his commentary on Romans. It, as has often been said, landed like a bombshell on the theological playground of Europe. It turned theological thinking around with a call to take the Bible seriously again. In his preface to the second edition, the edition translated into English, Barth replied to his critics in these words:

> When I am named "Biblicist," all that can rightly be proved against me is that I am prejudiced in supposing the Bible to be a good book, and that I hold it to be profitable for men to take its conceptions at least as seriously as they take their own.[11]

In the second half of the century, C. K. Barrett, an outstanding British New Testament scholar, wrote, "Barth's commentary I read as an undergraduate. If in those days, and since, I remained and have continued to be a Christian, I owe the fact in large measure to that book."[12]

After all these years and outstanding scholars, is anything left to say about Romans? I and other scholars find it nearly impossible to keep up with the scholarly, devotional, and sermonic output on the epistle. It continues to correct and instruct us at the beginning of the twenty-first century, and it will do so until the Lord's return.

For Further Reading

Anderson, R. Dean, Jr. *Ancient Rhetorical Theory and Paul.* Leuven, The Netherlands: Peeters, 1999.

Becker, Jurgen. *Paul: Apostle to the Gentiles.* Louisville: Westminster/John Knox Press, 1993.

Beker, J. Christiaan. *Paul the Apostle.* Philadelphia: Fortress Press, 1980.

Blumenfeld, B. *The Political Paul: Justice, Democracy and Kingship in a Hellenistic Framework.* JSNT Supplementary Series 210. London–New York: Sheffield Academic Press, 2001.

Bornkamm, Gunther. *Paul.* New York: Harper & Row, 1971.

Bruce, F. F. *Paul: Apostle of the Heart Set Free.* Grand Rapids: W. B. Eerdmans, 1977.

Donfried, Karl P. *The Romans Debate.* Minneapolis: Augsburg, 1977.

Dunn, James D. G. *Romans 1–8.* Word Biblical Commentary. Dallas: Word Books, 1988.

———. *Romans 9–16.* Word Biblical Commentary. Dallas: Word Books, 1988.

Ellis, E. Earle. *Paul and His Recent Interpreters.* Grand Rapids: W. B. Eerdmans, 1968.

Gamble, Harry, Jr. *The Textual History of the Letter to the Romans.* Grand Rapids: W. B. Eerdmans, 1977.

Goodspeed, Edgar J. *Paul.* Nashville & New York: Abingdon Press, 1947.

Grieb, A. Katherine. *The Story of Romans: A Narrative Defense of God's Righteousness.* Louisville: Westminster John Knox Press, 2002.

Gross, N. L. *If You Cannot Preach Like Paul...* Grand Rapids: W. B. Eerdmans, 2002.

Harink, D. *Paul among the Postliberals: Pauline Theology beyond Christendom and Modernity.* Grand Rapids: Brazos Press, 2003.

Hengel, Martin. *The Pre-Christian Paul.* Philadelphia: Trinity Press International, 1991.

Hooker, Morna D. *A Preface to Paul.* New York: Oxford University Press, 1980.

———. *Paul: A Short Introduction.* Oxford: Oneworld, 2003.

Jervis, L. Ann. *The Purpose of Romans: A Comparative Letter Structure Investigation.* Journal for the Study of the New Testament Supplement Series 55. Sheffield, England: JSOT Press, 1991.

Jones, P. *Capturing the Pagan Mind: Paul's Blueprint for Thinking and Living in the New Global Culture.* Nashville: Broadman and Holman, 2003.

Keck, Leander E. *Paul and His Letters.* Philadelphia: Fortress Press, 1979.

Knox, John. *Chapters in a Life of Paul.* Nashville: Abingdon–Cokesbury Press, 1946.

Lapide, Pinchas, and Peter Stuhlmacher. *Paul: Rabbi and Apostle.* Minneapolis: Augsburg, 1981.

Longenecker, Richard N. *Paul: Apostle of Liberty.* Grand Rapids: Baker Book House, 1977.

——. *The Road from Damascus.* Grand Rapids: W. B. Eerdmans, 1997.

Luedemann, Gerd. *Paul, Apostle to the Gentiles: Studies in Chronology.* Translated by F. Stanley Jones. Philadelphia: Fortress Press, 1984 (German ed., 1980).

——. *Paul The Founder of Christianity.* Amherst, N.Y.: Prometheus, 2002 (German ed., 2001).

MacDonald, Dennis Ronald. *The Legend and The Apostle.* Philadelphia: The Westminster Press, 1983.

Machen, J. Gresham. *The Origin of Paul's Religion.* Grand Rapids: W. B. Eerdmans, 1978.

McRay, J. *Paul: His Life and Teaching.* Grand Rapids: Baker, 2003.

Meeks, Wayne A. *The First Urban Christians.* New Haven, Conn., and London: Yale University Press, 1983.

Moo, D. J. *Encountering the Book of Romans: A Theological Survey.* Grand Rapids: Baker, 2002.

Murphy-O'Connor, Jerome. *Paul: A Critical Life.* Oxford: Clarendon Press, 1996.

——. *Paul the Letter-Writer: His World, His Options, His Skills.* Collegeville, Minn.: Michael Glazier/ The Liturgical Press, 1995.

Pedersen, Troels Engberg. *Paul in His Hellenistic Context.* Minneapolis: Fortress Press, 1995.

Polhill, John B. *Paul and His Letters.* Nashville: Broadman and Holman, 1999.

Pollock, John. *The Apostle: A Life of Paul.* Garden City: Doubleday & Company, 1969.

Ramsay, W. M. *St. Paul the Traveller and the Roman Citizen.* Grand Rapids: Baker, 1979.

Richards, Hubert. *Reading Paul Today.* Atlanta: John Knox Press, 1980.

Roetzel, Calvin. *Paul: The Man and the Myth.* Minneapolis: Fortress Press, 1999.

Schweitzer, Albert. *Paul and His Interpreters.* New York: Schocken, 1991.

Segal, Alan F. *Paul the Convert.* New Haven, Conn., and London: Yale University Press, 1990.

Stendahl, Krister. *Paul Among Jews and Gentiles.* Philadelphia: Fortress Press, 1987.

Stewart, James S. *A Man in Christ.* New York: Harper and Brothers, 1935.

Talbert, C. H. *Romans.* Smyth & Helwys Bible Commentary. Macon, Ga.: Smyth & Helwys, 2002.

Wedderburn, A. J. M. *The Reasons for Romans.* Minneapolis: Fortress Press, 1991.

Westerholm, Stephen. *Preface to the Study of Paul.* Grand Rapids: W. B. Eerdmans, 1997.

Wilson, A. N. *Paul: The Mind of the Apostle.* New York: W. W. Norton & Company, 1997.

Witherington, Ben, III. *Paul's Narrative Thought World.* Louisville: Westminster John Knox Press, 1994.

PART 1

Major Issues or Themes of Romans

CHAPTER 1

What Romans Says about Preaching

1:1–5

Paul, a servant of Jesus Christ, called to be an apostle, set apart for the gospel of God, which he promised beforehand through his prophets in the holy scriptures, the gospel concerning his Son, who was descended from David according to the flesh and was declared to be Son of God with power according to the spirit of holiness by resurrection from the dead, Jesus Christ our Lord, through whom we have received grace and apostleship to bring about the obedience of faith among all the Gentiles for the sake of his name.

Paul was a church planter—indeed. His strategy for planting the church of Jesus Christ wherever he traveled was to preach and teach the gospel. He identified himself here as one "set apart for the gospel of God." In making this identification, Paul connected himself and his mission with the scriptural prophets and with God's resurrected Son, "Jesus Christ our Lord." He will become more specific in chapter 10 about these scriptural and christological connections. Here he apparently refers to understandings that he held in common with the believers in Rome and presumably believers everywhere, confidence in the authority of the Hebrew Scriptures and in the common belief in Jesus as Son of God, Christ, and Lord as shown in the resurrection. The wording of verses 3 and 4 are so odd for Paul that many scholars assume he was using a familiar creedal statement with which the Roman Christians would have immediately agreed.

And what is the gospel? The rest of the epistle answers that question at least as to content. However, it is important for us to understand that for Paul, as for all early Christians, the gospel was something to be communicated orally, that is, to be preached and taught. Those earliest Christians would have had great difficulty thinking about the gospel as independent of its being spoken. Even the four books designated gospels in our New Testament were recorded after many years of the telling of their stories. The written gospels were intended to be read aloud in their oral culture.

Literature was seen not only as an important way to record the spoken word for posterity. Literature transported the spoken word across geographical, cultural, and political boundaries. Still, the spoken word remained the primary form of human communication. Today, billboards, books, newspapers, and magazines surround us. Script fills our computer and television screens. Thus we find it hard to appreciate how language worked in a culture where no more than ten percent of the population could read. The gospel was inseparable from speech.

1:16–17

> For I am not ashamed of the gospel; it is the power of God for salvation to everyone who has faith, to the Jew first and also to the Greek. For in it the righteousness of God is revealed through faith for faith; as it is written, "The one who is righteous will live by faith."

This statement opens the essay section of Paul's epistle and functions as a theme statement for the whole epistle and as a pointer to the central focus of Paul's life and ministry. These two verses should never be separated. The statement is a natural outgrowth of what has gone before since verse 15 ends with Paul's wish to proclaim the gospel (*euangelisasthai*) in Rome as he had been doing among people elsewhere. Verses 16 and 17 are personal words that set the theme for the rest of the epistle.

As a theme statement, each part is important. It begins with a personal testimony, continues with a brief justification of the testimony, goes on to describe the scope of gospel power, and ends with a text from the prophet Habakkuk (2:4).

For Paul to say that he was not ashamed of the gospel is equivalent to his saying he would openly proclaim the gospel everywhere he could get a hearing. What we know about Paul's life indicates his was no empty boast. He was apparently ready to risk all to preach the gospel.

Why would a person run such a risk? It was and is a God thing. When he claimed that the gospel "is the power of God for salvation," Paul did not identify some magical property of the message. Rather, he witnessed that in his experience, preaching that message unleashed a powerful process attributable only to God. That preaching somehow effected the salvation of those who responded to it in faith.

In addition to salvation, Paul added, in the gospel, "the righteousness of God is revealed." Divine revelation is an astounding claim for a human being to make. Of course, Paul and believers everywhere knew about prophets who claimed to speak the word of the Lord. So Paul insisted that preaching the gospel (not only his preaching but the gospel in general) was part of the process of God's revealing God's own nature. As if the claim to the power that leads to salvation were not enough, Paul connected preaching with the ongoing revelation of God to the human race.

So Paul, at the beginning of his epistle, put great weight on the gospel. What did he have in mind with his use of this term? We often overlook the fact that the word *gospel* appears nearly exclusively in Paul's writings. It appears, in one of four forms, eighty-four times in Pauline literature, while being used only seventy times in the rest of the New Testament and the writings of the early church fathers. In Galatians 1 and 2, Paul treats the gospel as an identifiable body of teaching that could be contrasted with "another gospel" or with no gospel at all. In 1 Corinthians 15, he defines *gospel* in terms of the facts of Jesus' death, burial, resurrection, and appearances. Here in Romans, he describes it as the power for salvation and as a vehicle for God's self-revelation.

Paul's use of the word *gospel* includes the whole scope of his life as a Christian. It refers to his own experience of conversion and commission on the road to Damascus. It embraces all the new historical and doctrinal thinking he had to do as a result of that event. It points to the reality of Jesus as the dominant fact of all history. It defines Paul's own lifework as a missionary. And it describes the results of his preaching, not only in terms of individual conversion but also as the fulfillment of the expectation of the whole Hebrew Bible that the kingdom or covenant of God would be opened to all the nations of the earth. Paul's good news was that in Christ God's promise to Abraham (Gen. 12:3; 18:18; 22:18)–the promise that all the nations of the Earth would be blessed through Abraham's offspring–was being fulfilled. This leads Paul to describe the scope of gospel power in the statement, "to the Jew first and also to the Greek" (Rom. 1:16). Without arrogance, Paul described himself as the major proclaimer of this good news to the nations.

We shall postpone our investigation of Paul's use of the theme of righteousness and justification to chapter 3, but 1:17 presents us with an interesting challenge in interpreting Paul. What the NRSV renders "the righteousness of God is revealed through faith for faith," the NIV translates "a righteousness that is by faith from first to last." The Greek text reads literally "righteousness is revealed from faith to faith." Many translators and commentators understand this phrase to be Paul's way of saying what Martin Luther made explicit in his phrase "by faith alone." Keeping in mind the primary Hebrew meaning of faith as faithfulness and as often referring to God (see Rom. 3:3), we could translate these words "from [God's] faithfulness to [our] faith." This is, after all, the direction of the gospel and the actual wording of the sentence.

The passage closes with the quotation of Habakkuk 2:4, "The one who is righteous will live by faith" (author's translation). The Hebrew reads: "the righteous one will live by his or her own faith or faithfulness." The Septuagint, the earliest Greek translation (LXX), says, "the righteous shall live by God's faithfulness or by faith in God" (the pronoun is "my" or "of me"). Paul deleted a pronoun when he quoted this verse. This avoids the question of which pronoun—third person or first person—was originally in the text and leaves the statement general enough to stand as a thematic text for the rest of the book. As it stands, Paul's Greek could be translated "The one who is righteous by faith will live." This forms a good outline for the rest of the epistle with chapters 1–11 showing how a person becomes righteous by faith and chapters 12–16 dealing with how to live on that basis.

So, in chapter 1, Paul makes it clear that the gospel is God's message and that God means it for us. God is the only one who could make good news possible for sinful humanity. As God's good news, the gospel is the revelation of God. It was not what people were expecting. The proclamation of Jesus Christ caught Jews and Gentiles alike off guard. It was not a message of human wisdom or philosophy. In fact, as Paul wrote in 1 Corinthians 1 and 2, the wise of his day laughed at the gospel as foolishness. The gospel was not a new list of legal demands. Christ's teaching and his crucifixion caused something of a crisis in connection with the law. The gospel was a new view of God, a God of righteousness who takes the seemingly unrighteous step of justifying the wicked (Rom. 4:5).

As God's good news, the gospel is the Son of God himself (Rom. 1:9). It is not a book of deep thinking as important as that can be. It is not a list of instructions as much as we humans need that. It is not even a good example since it centers on the incarnate God, a status none of us can attain. The gospel is the life, death, and resurrection of Jesus Christ our Lord. Our thinking about him is important. His teachings for us are important. And our aspiring to live as he did is important. Most important is what he has done for our salvation, which we could not have accomplished for ourselves.

As God's good news, the gospel is the purpose of God (Rom. 1:5). By this, I understand Paul to mean the gospel reveals God's will, and it is the major instrument for accomplishing that gracious will. God's purpose is not limited; the gospel is for everybody—Jews and Greeks. In the gospel God's redemption is offered. That means the gospel is designed to awaken faith, the acceptance of the truth of the good news and personal submission to the God it reveals. Such faith is necessary for receiving that redemption. The new reality of faith lives and grows in the process of obedience to the continual hearing of the gospel. Thus, the purpose of God seems to be, at least for the present, tied totally to the gospel.

As God's good news, the gospel is the power of God. We too often denigrate words as being weak. "That's just talk," we say; or "Talk is cheap." But God's talk created the universe; so God's message does not consist of weak words. The powerful word of the resurrection, by which God's Spirit declared Jesus to be the Son of God, is the same power that accomplishes the salvation of every believer.

The gospel is wholly God's, but Paul can call it "my gospel" (Rom. 2:16). It is the good news of God for us. Paul will state what is for us Christians an almost commonplace statement about Christ in Romans 4:25, "who was handed over to death for our trespasses and was raised for our justification." Redemption, salvation, atonement, reconciliation, and—for Paul the greatest of this vocabulary—justification, are all terms indicating that we human beings are in a bad way and cannot improve our lot without God's help. In other words, from our standpoint any consideration of the gospel must begin with the awareness of sin, which is precisely where Paul begins his gospel logic. The gospel is for our sins. God's good news is for us also because it is given for our hearing. It is put in our human language. Now that is a risky business, because we have misunderstood and been misunderstood even in communication with those who are closest to us. But God is consistent. God made salvation possible by becoming one of us, and God makes salvation available by offering it in human language. Furthermore, the form of that language is not just propositions, explanations, rules, or reprimands. The form of that language is narrative. Yes, gospel language is the story of Jesus, language that goes beyond the intellect to the heart.

God's good news is for us because God sends it for the obedience of our faith. The response God expects from those who really hear the gospel is believing accompanied by obeying the Lord. The usual initial act of obedience is immersion in water, the meaning of which Paul discusses in Romans 6:1–14.

The expected response to the gospel is not doctrinal, technical, or physically demanding. Thus, all of us can obey.

When we witness the baptism of a person with severe mental or physical challenges and note the thrill of the moment for that person, the importance of this aspect of the gospel strikes us. Yes, anyone can follow Jesus in the initial act of obedience. It should cause us to praise God for God's great mercy. An aspect closely related to this is the fact that the gospel is not forced on anybody. It is offered to us all in terms to which we can relate, leaving us free to make or reject the decision of faith.

God's good news is for our salvation. As we shall see, especially in 5:1–11 and in chapters 4 and 11, this means more than the future deliverance of our souls from God's wrath though that is included. God's gospel heals life in its totality. It offers security, encouragement, hope, and meaning for life here and hereafter.

Finally, God's good news is for our proclamation. This is perhaps the most surprising and frightening aspect of the gospel. God runs the risk of entrusting the gospel to us, the sinners who needed it in the first place. This points to the general risk of putting the message in human language and to the specific risk of leaving it to you and me, of all people, to communicate it. As far as we know, God has no plan B. Thus, the church is always one generation from extinction. As foolish as that may seem (see 1 Cor. 1:21), it has worked more or less effectively for nearly two thousand years. Since the days of Peter and Paul, God has used unpromising people to accomplish great things. We believe that God is still capable of doing that and is doing it. God needs only our willingness and our cooperation to tell the story to the best of our ability. God has created and empowered the gospel so we can pass it on to others.

These are big claims about preaching. They are worth our careful and prayerful consideration.

9:1, 6

I am speaking the truth in Christ—I am not lying; my conscience confirms it by the Holy Spirit…It is not as though the word of God had failed.

These verses are not usually considered in a study of Paul's preaching, but they seem to me to be significant, especially since they appear in a very emotional passage. Paul rarely resorted to taking an oath, but this passage is an exception. Verse 1 opens three chapters that many have suggested could stand alone. Might they be a hint at least of Paul's synagogue preaching? The three chapters deal with a question he asked in 3:1–"*Then what advantage has the Jew? Or what is the value of circumcision?*" He began to answer his question there with "*Much, in every way. For in the first place the Jews were entrusted with the oracles of God.*" In chapter 9, he returned to that question, offering more answers. The conundrum behind all this is that most Jews had rejected Jesus as their messiah. Paul had persecuted Christians and was turned around only by a special revelation of the risen Lord. What this meant about God, about God's word, and about the status of Israel as God's chosen ones was bothersome, especially in a situation such as the one in Rome, where Jewish and Gentile Christians were living together. We shall return to this issue in later chapters.

For now let us notice how important it was to Paul to have his words trusted. This remains true for all Christians. Since we are a people of the word, since our faith is based on hearing testimony, and since our task as preachers is to present the gospel convincingly, credibility is central to our identity and commission. The other side of the coin of credibility is the word that we speak. When Paul affirmed that God's word had not failed, he dealt with a central aspect of the gospel's power. Preaching the word is vital; but hearing it produces faith. The hearer is always an active agent in the communication process.

We preachers would like to think we control the preaching moment, but Paul indicates that even God does not have total control over the efficacy of communication. God's word does not fail, but at the same time, some people do reject it. Paul at times talked in terms of God's hardening hearts, as in chapter 9, where he discusses Pharaoh. However, Paul holds humans responsible for their own decisions to reject God's will. Romans 1:18–32 graphically describes the fall of humanity into the life of sin. The blame lies at the feet of those who "though they knew God, they did not honor him as God or give thanks to him, but they became futile in their thinking, and their senseless minds were darkened" (v. 21). Paul prefaces this description with the words, "So they are without excuse."

This point of tension in Paul's thinking has bothered theologians and divided Christians through two millennia, but preachers must endure the tension. Sometimes, we eventually see God's will working out because of temporary rejection or negative reactions. Other times we never see that. All we can do is follow Paul's lead. When the subject is God, Paul talks in terms of total sovereignty. When the subject is his fellow human beings, Paul talks in terms of total responsibility. Such tension should not debilitate us any more than it did Paul. It should act as a creative dialectic. The cliché, "Pray as though everything depends on God and work as though everything depends on you," lives on because it states clearly the creative tension in which preachers and other Christians live. But in our next passage, Paul points to a third aspect of the communication process that is always present: the hearer.

10:5–21

Moses writes concerning the righteousness that comes from the law, that "the person who does these things will live by them." But the righteousness that comes from faith says, "Do not say in your heart, 'Who will ascend into heaven?'" (that is, to bring Christ down) "or 'Who will descend into the abyss?'" (that is, to bring Christ up from the dead). But what does it say?

"The word is near you,
    on your lips and in your heart"

(that is, the word of faith that we proclaim); because if you confess with your lips that Jesus is Lord and believe in your heart that God raised him from the dead, you will be saved. For one believes with the heart and so is justified, and one confesses with the mouth and so is saved. The scripture says, "No one who believes in him will be put to shame." For there is no distinction between Jew and Greek; the same Lord is Lord of all and is generous to all who call on him. For, "Everyone who calls on the name of the Lord shall be saved."

But how are they to call on one in whom they have not believed? And how are they to believe in one of whom they have never heard? And how are they to hear without someone to proclaim him? And how are they to proclaim him unless they are sent? As it is written, "How beautiful are the feet of those who bring good news!" But not all have obeyed the good news; for Isaiah says, "Lord, who has believed our message?" So faith comes from what is heard, and what is heard comes through the word of Christ.

But I ask, have they not heard? Indeed they have; for

"Their voice has gone out to all the earth,

and their words to the ends of the world."

Again I ask, did Israel not understand? First Moses says,

"I will make you jealous of those who are not a
nation;

with a foolish nation I will make you angry."

Then Isaiah is so bold as to say,

"I have been found by those who did not seek me;

I have shown myself to those who did not ask
for me."

But of Israel he says, "All day long I have held out my hands to a disobedient and contrary people."

I chose to quote all seventeen verses here because I see them as a unit, a unit that reveals much about Paul's understanding of preaching. He begins with a reference to Moses. This is typical of rabbinic midrash. This rabbinic method for studying scripture normally treats a *torah* text first and then another biblical text (called *haphtarah*). It combines them to explain each other and the issue at hand. Paul's immediate issue is the tension between legal righteousness and righteousness by faith. For the present I am more interested in *how* Paul argues than in *what* he argues. For more details on this passage, see chapter 14.

Notice how quickly Paul begins to quote the words of Moses from Deuteronomy 30. These are the last words Moses spoke to the people of Israel before they marched into the promised land and before Moses climbed Mount Nebo to die. Thus, they carried great emotional weight for Jews of Paul's day. In this context, heavily weighted with concern for Israel, Paul in a sense puts himself in the place of Moses, whose words he quotes. Paul's explanatory comments, inserted into the text *pesher*-style[1] make an immediate Christian application. Moses warned the Israelites not to seek God anywhere other than in the word from God that was already theirs. Paul implies that legalistic righteousness is tantamount to trying to find or win something the people of God already have. A further implication is that the Christian who tries to win his or her own salvation is ignoring the significance of both the incarnation and the resurrection. Christ has already come from heaven and has already risen from the dead. Any attempt to earn the gift Christ has already given to us is at best foolish and at worst idolatrous.

In verses 11–13, Paul completes this point by quoting two prophets, Isaiah 28:16 and Joel 2:32. From them, he arrives at the universal consequences of the gospel: "there is no distinction between Jew and Greek" (v. 12). Once again, Paul in one statement shows the implications of his argument and points to another theme with which he has to deal more fully—the relationship of Jew and Gentile in the reign of God.

First he has to complete another line of thought. This idea commands this passage and is highlighted by the Joel quotation, the means of evangelism. Joel promised salvation to "Everyone who calls on the name of the LORD" (Joel 2:32). Paul follows this up with a series of questions that leads the reader to a consideration of the place of preaching and the preacher in the plan of God. The logic here seems so obvious that it is amazing how often we ignore it.

Throughout its history, the church has produced thinkers and leaders who have become so enamored of one or another truth of the gospel that they tend to neglect other truths. Some say "faith alone" is the means of salvation. Others say "grace alone." Others say baptism, church activities, or good living. Paul's series of questions should remind us that no one aspect of the plan of salvation stands alone. He had established that its efficacy depends on the death and resurrection of Christ (see Rom. 4:25), the greatest gift of God's grace. Here, he claimed that "one confesses with the mouth and so is saved" (Rom. 10:10). This shows a progression of dependencies: confession is dependent on faith, faith is dependent on hearing, hearing is dependent on speaking, and speaking in this case is dependent on being commissioned.

Faith is not some miraculous gift. Faith is the response of the thinking person to what that person hears. The message does not come in a voice from the clouds; it is borne by a human messenger. That messenger does not dream up the message on his or her own. The message is given and sent by its giver. All is from God, but it is all by means of human beings. Verse 15 closes with the stirring description from Isaiah 52:7, "How beautiful are the feet of those who bring good news!"

That, of course, poses a problem. If it is possible for any person to hear and believe to be saved, why do some hear but refuse to believe? Why is it that "not all have obeyed the good news"? In response to this question, Paul (v. 16) quotes Isaiah 53:1, "Lord, who has believed our message?" This indicates that the problem was not new in Paul's age. One could wish that Paul's answer were clearer. Verse 17 is often quoted but rarely explained: "So faith comes from what is heard, and what is heard comes through the word of Christ." "Message" (v. 16) and "what is heard" (v. 17) translate the Greek word *akoe* a term taken over from the Greek (LXX) translation of Isaiah 53:1. The Hebrew *shamu`ah*, in Isaiah, has the same Hebrew root as the familiar Hebrew word *shema`*, the opening of the Jewish call to worship and confession of faith: "Hear, O Israel, the LORD our God, the LORD is one" (Deut. 6:4, NIV). So Paul taps into the heart of the Jewish faith in this whole context. He quotes Moses' final words and continues by bringing in Joel and Isaiah. Finally, he teaches that just as the first responsibility of the Israelite is to "hear," so also with the Christian. Saving faith–justifying faith–comes from hearing.

Another connection is the similarity of Paul's words for hearing and obeying. The term *akoe* is the root of the term for obedience, *hypakoe,* following the Old Testament sense of *shema`,* to hear or obey. In 1:5, Paul said the intended end of his preaching is the "obedience of faith." In 10:16, he pointed out that "not all have obeyed the good news." He now closes the epistle (16:26) with the hope of the "obedience of faith."

Can we draw a conclusion from all these connections? We can say, at least, that Paul expected saving faith to grow out of the kind of hearing of the gospel that issued in obedience. But he was not finished, and neither are we. This *akoe,* he says, is through (*dia*) the word of Christ.[2] We are reminded that the success of the preaching of the gospel comes not from our expertise as preachers. If we are responsible ministers of the word, we will be the best communicators possible. However, the ultimate outcome is by another means "the word of Christ." After all, nobody is ready to obey every word heard. The word we obey is the word we recognize as coming from God or Christ.

The Greek language has several ways of saying the same thing. Many Christians who have not studied Greek have heard that the Greek term for "word" is *logos.* That is true. *Logos* is used in the opening of John's gospel and elsewhere to describe Jesus and the message about Jesus. However, here Paul uses an alternate term, *rhema.* This is the term the Greek translation (LXX) used in Moses' speech (Deut. 30:12–14) that Paul quotes in verse 8. This "word" is not so much a grand message as a personal utterance. Paul did not indicate that the production of faith is dependent on the gullibility of the listeners nor on the persuasiveness of the preacher. He did indicate that Christ himself is involved. It is the word–the utterance–of Christ that is the decisive factor in this process. Thus, effective preaching/hearing depends on the preacher's clarity and faithfulness, the audience's willingness to pay attention and take the message to heart, and Christ's active participation. We can assume that Christ is present where the gospel is being communicated (see Mt. 28:20). The effectiveness of preaching the gospel depends on the faithfulness of us who preach it and on the consecrated attention of those who listen to it.

Paul returns to the concrete question of Israel's rejection of Christ. He puts it two ways: "Have they not heard?" (v. 18) and "Did Israel not understand?" (v. 19). In verses 18–21, he addresses these questions by presenting a series of quotations from all three of the major divisions of the Hebrew Bible: Law, Prophets, and Writings. He begins in the third division, with Psalm 19. This psalm opens with a poetic description: the physical creation, that is, the universe, proclaims God's greatness. The psalm's second half deals with the word of God. Israel has heard, Paul argues, in the sense of being exposed to the revelation. But has Israel really paid attention? Deuteronomy 32:21 then set up an argument that Paul develops in chapter 11, indicating that God is somehow at work in Israel's rejecting their Messiah. Words from Isaiah 65 make clear that Israel has not understood because Israel is "a disobedient and contrary people." Paul clarifies that the kind of hearing (*akoe*) that produces saving faith is attention to the word with the intent of obeying what is recognized as a divine mandate.

Conclusion

For Paul, preaching is a high privilege, especially since it is left to sinful human beings. It is a privilege to be involved in the communication that becomes God's power for salvation. It is a privilege to say a word that becomes the expression of Christ. It is a privilege to speak to elicit faith in hearers. It puts preachers in a line of God's servants reaching back to Moses and coming down through the prophets and apostles. It is hard work, as Paul well knew, but there is no more important or deeply satisfying work a human being can do.

For Further Reading

Beaudean, John William, Jr. *Paul's Theology of Preaching.* Macon, Ga.: Mercer University Press, 1988.

Gilliland, Dean S. *Pauline Theology & Mission Practice.* Grand Rapids: Baker, 1983.

Gross, Nancy. *If You Cannot Preach Like Paul.* Grand Rapids: W. B. Eerdmans, 2002.

Hafemann, Scott J. *Suffering and Ministry in the Spirit.* Grand Rapids: W. B. Eerdmans, 1990.

Hultgren, Arland J. *Paul's Gospel and Mission.* Philadelphia: Fortress Press, 1985.

Longenecker, Richard N. *The Ministry and Message of Paul.* Grand Rapids: Zondervan, 1980.

Murphy-O'Conner, Jerome. *Paul on Preaching.* New York: Sheed and Ward, 1964.

Patte, Daniel. *Paul's Faith and the Power of the Gospel.* Philadelphia: Fortress Press, 1983.

Thompson, James. *Preaching Like Paul: Homiletical Wisdom for Today.* Louisville: Westminster John Knox Press, 2000.

CHAPTER 2

What Romans Says about Creation[1]

Revelation in nature appears first in the negative context of Romans 1:18–24. This revelation of God's wrath is an indictment charging the whole human race with sin. We find no instance of the theme of natural revelation appearing in a positive context, although the law "written on their hearts" (2:14–16) can be read as having positive implications. Even Acts 17 uses revelation in creation to point to the need of forgiveness. At the same time, we must recognize that this positive side of general revelation exists. We cannot escape it, and it is unfair to explain it away. The works of creation are seen as one means that God uses to reveal something of divinity.[2] Apparently Paul used revelation in nature as a point of contact with the Gentiles in preparation for the further revelation in word. We see this in the Areopagus sermon in Acts 17, but it is also apparent in Romans 1. In Romans 1, Paul sets out to show the universal need of justification. He argues that every person is responsible before God for his or her sinful state. Thus, revelation in nature is a positive affirmation used for a positive purpose but always in a context of negative discourse.

Anthropological themes also are used negatively. In Romans 5 and 7, humans are seen as weak and under control of sin. The fault is never God's, as in the rabbinic texts that identify both good and evil impulses as parts of original creation. Paul portrays sin as a powerful interloper. Sin is a power independent of God that invades the world by attacking individuals at their weakest point, the flesh. Sin's entrance into the world (seen universally in Rom. 5 and individually in Rom. 7) caused a fundamental change in every person's created nature: the loss of God's glory (Rom. 3:23). As a result, Paul described humans as responsible for their actions while simultaneously helpless to resist the power of sin. Thus, the individual on his or her own is only miserable.

This misery that Paul described in Romans 7 comes when the individual tries to keep God's law with merely human power. The law appears in two different lights in Romans. Positively, the law is God's order for life. Negatively, at least from Paul's Christian perspective (cf. 2 Cor. 3:9–11), the law lacks the power to reorder a person's life which has fallen into the disorder of sin. Romans 12 points out that this same order is fulfilled and made possible in the new creation in Christ. This offers a probable connecting point with Paul's term *nomos Christou* (law of Christ) in Galatians 6:2 (cf. 1 Cor. 9:21).

For Paul, new creation is the result of justification. In Romans, as in Galatians 3:21, *dikaiosyne* (justification/righteousness) is defined in terms of *zoopoiein* (creating life). Sanday and Headlam have pointed to the forensic use of *dikaiosyne*[3] But Paul added a factor to this courtroom scene. The Judge is the Creator, as Paul pointed out in Romans 4 (see chapter 10). If we forget this, we miss the thrust of Paul's discourses on justification. He made this explicit in 2 Corinthians 4:6, but it is implicit each time Paul deals with *dikaiosyne* as an act of God. He could hardly have imagined God's making a pronouncement that would be exclusively forensic. When the Creator speaks, something happens.

Therefore, the justified person is not only reckoned righteous, but *becomes* and *is* righteous. A real change happens in God's act of justification. This explains how Paul could deal so loftily with the simple rite of baptism in Romans 6. Time and distance do not set limits for the Creator. The justification of the individual that takes place at baptism involves participation in the past death, burial, and resurrection of Christ. Justification effects a real and radical change in the individual in the present and offers evidence for the belief in the eschatological resurrection to life. Romans 8:29–30 could have been an early baptismal formula bringing together, as it does foreknowledge, election, justification, and glorification in a chapter descriptive of the new creation.

Paul also deals with the material cosmos in eschatological settings. Romans 2:14–16 is a peculiar text in several ways. It stands in the context of Paul's argument that all humans are sinners and are, therefore, in need of God's grace. It makes this a part of Paul's argument with a reference to God's judgment day. Thus it deals with both sin and eschatology by making a claim about human nature. Paul always considered human nature to be a result of God's creation. Look carefully at these three verses:

> When Gentiles, who do not possess the law, do instinctively what the law requires, these, though not having the law, are a law to themselves. They show that what the law requires is written on their hearts, to which their own conscience also bears witness; and their conflicting thoughts will accuse or perhaps excuse them on the day when, according to my gospel, God, through Jesus Christ, will judge the secret thoughts of all.

Paul insists he does not intend to speak of all Gentiles (*ethne*) but only of those Gentiles who fit his description: those "who do not possess the law, [but] do instinctively what the law requires." Those not having the *Torah* are, of course, all persons outside the confines of Judaism. The meaning of *physei* (instinctively or by nature) here depends on whether one connects it with *echonta* (having) or with *poiosin* (do). In the first case, *physei* means those who by nature or birth do not have the law.[4] In the second case, it refers to the instinctive doing of the law's demands. Though Paul customarily uses *physis* to refer to the status of birth, the rest of this passage appears to demand that we, as in the translation above, connect *physei* with *poiosin* in the Stoic sense of natural law.[5]

Paul claims that some Gentiles instinctively obey the *Torah.* They "are a law to themselves." Here Paul seems to stand far removed from the Old Testament claim for the exclusiveness of the *Torah.* He introduces *nomos* (law) in chapter 2 to show the universal applicability of God's righteous judgment.[6] To accomplish this, he has to do in relation to the law what he did in chapter 1 in relation to revelation, that is, show that Jew and Gentile are equally responsible. The concept *nomos* is a common Old Testament theme, but to use it in a statement such as "do instinctively what the law requires" seems specifically Hellenistic with the Stoics having absolutized *nomos* by limiting it to cases where *nomos* and *physis* agree.[7]

To go further and claim they are a law to themselves takes another step away from the Old Testament. Some scholars have hinted this is a direct quotation from Platonic Aristotelian philosophy; at any rate the idea is found there.[8] Philo went so far as to apply this concept to Abraham.[9] The concept of a law written on their hearts is a good Greek motif. Paul's language is akin to Jeremiah 31:33. Admittedly, Jeremiah deals only with Israel; nevertheless, he represents a step away from the total dependence on the written law that characterizes so much of the Old Testament thinking. Perhaps even more to the point is the advice of Proverbs 3:1–4, to "let your heart keep my commandments" (v. 1) and to write love and faithfulness "on the tablet of your heart" (v. 3). Paul has declared that Jews and non-Jews have received God's law[10] and will be judged by God on the basis of how they have lived in relation to that law. To make this pronouncement, Paul is willing to mix the Stoic tradition of *lex naturae* (natural law) with his Jewish traditions, changing the emphasis of both in the process.[11]

Verse 15 shows that Paul understands this state of affairs not as though the Gentiles naturally worked things out among themselves but that an internal kind of law was given (cf. Wis. 7:22ff. and 9:17–19). If the work or requirement of the law is written on the hearts of people, there would be some sort of inner recognition of obedience and/or disobedience. *Kardia* (heart) in Pauline anthropology is the center of both reason and will as well as (as is clear here) the place where God's law is written.[12]

Paul proceeds to identify the inner recognition mechanisms in two genitive absolutes. The first names the conscience as witnessing with or to the person, and the second names the reasoning facility as sometimes accusing and sometimes defending not only within the individual, but also between individuals (*metaxu allelon*). The terms *syneidesis* (conscience) and *logismos* (thoughts) were common to Paul's contemporary Greek and Roman authors. They were, however, foreign to the canonical Hebrew Bible although the awareness of the phenomena is clear in some uses of the word *heart*[13] and of the concept of the good influence.[14]

Paul's contemporaries would have understood the use of *conscience* here, even though it differed from their philosophical thought.[15] Seneca used conscience as a final authority. Philo identified it with God's own word.[16] But "Paul took *syneidesis* with a comprehensive breadth and variety not found in any of his predecessors...It has now become the central self-consciousness of knowing and acting man."[17] Thus, Paul can both deal with negative functions of conscience (cf. 1 Cor. 8:7–13 and 2 Cor. 1:12) and, as here, elevate conscience to play a role (along with reason) in preparing the individual for the final judgment.[18]

An instructive parallel to this thought appears in 1 Enoch 63:1–9, a vision of the final judgment of "the mighty and the kings who possess the earth." They are judged unrighteous, and in that day they recognize and confess that they should have believed and glorified God. In verses 4, 5, and 7, they say: [19]

> We have now learnt that we should glorify and bless the Lord of kings and Him who is king over all kings.... Would that we had rest to glorify and give thanks and confess our faith before His glory!... For we have not believed before Him nor glorified the name of the Lord of Spirits.

This eschatological function of the conscience and reason sets our passage apart from the Old Testament and the Stoic or popular philosophy of its day, but it shows no gulf between Paul and at least some of his Jewish contemporaries.

If one permits these two verses to speak for themselves, one must admit that Paul at least gives a nod toward the Stoic concept of natural law to confirm the fact of moral living among peoples who had no access to God's written law. But he put the statement in a context of responsibility before God and ultimate answerability in the judgment. Thus, this "law written in their hearts" is God's law, a part of God's revelation. It is to be held in tension with God's direct action in history, and ultimately it is subject to the lordship of Jesus Christ proclaimed in Paul's gospel.

Intertestamental literature and the later Old Testament books provide enough links between the ancient tradition of the *Torah* inscribed on stone and Paul's law written in the heart that we need not seek outside Jewish literature for sources for Paul's claim here. In fact, Jewish wisdom literature exhibited a strong tendency to identify the *Torah* and the general order of creation and society as a single revelation of and from God. This shows how Paul would have come to the position he here elucidates and how original readers would have been able to understand his statement.[20] At the same time we must recognize the peculiar stamp of Christian theology that marks Paul's statements—Christ Jesus both justifies and will judge.

In Romans 8, Paul presents the physical creation as sharing the results of human sin and as hoping to share the results of human redemption, that is, glorification. So in Paul, as in Genesis 3, the sorry state of the creation is seen as the fault of sinful humans. Similarly, the ultimate redemption of the creation awaits the completion of humankind's redemption. We certainly do not have here an attempt to develop a systematic statement on ecology. To claim, as did Bultmann, that Paul had no interest in the creation as such is to overlook the broad scope of his soteriology and eschatology. We must grant that Paul's first concern was the reconciliation of persons to God (2 Cor. 5:11–21). His faith in God as the Creator of all (*ta panta*) led him to consider the physical cosmos and to accord it a place in his theology.

The role spiritual beings other than the divinity played in this whole scene remains ambiguous. It is not just difficult to interpret, but clearly ambiguous. Paul never deals with the question of their origin, but he says that some of them are rebelling against God. Sin is treated as an alien power that can dominate an individual (Rom. 5:12–7:25). But the apostle assures his readers that God's act of redemption in Christ has broken the power of these beings. The resurrection and exaltation of Christ have made him Lord of even those rebellious powers, but they have not yet totally submitted themselves to him. Therefore, the spiritual beings still have to be reckoned with in this life. Each individual believer must submit to Christ and reject the other powers. We can assume Paul would have felt comfortable with the statement in 1 John 4:4 that "the one who is in you is greater than the one who is in the world." As Aulen points out, each time Paul deals with spiritual beings, he does so in a context full of the love of God in Christ.[21]

Conclusion

This investigation has shown the creation to be an important theme of Paul's theology. However, it is not a major issue in his gospel. Paul cannot be called a creation theologian. Jesus Christ is clearly central with his redemption and his lordship. But creation thinking does form a foundation on which Paul builds his theology. It is like bedrock, for the most part hidden but showing through the surface at certain strategic points. The most vital of these points is its comprising part of the paradigm that determines Paul's conception of God. God is defined not only in terms of creation, but his being Creator is never forgotten. This demands the understanding of justification in terms of the new creation.

Given this substructure of theology, Paul's faith in Christ had to be related to creation. We find direct lines connecting Christ with original and ongoing creation. His act of redemption is focused to an extent both on the new creation and on the renewal of the cosmos. The hope a Christian has in Christ is shared with the universe. The quality of Christian living is influenced both negatively and positively by elements of and awareness of the creation. So christology, soteriology, eschatology, and ethics are combined in Paul's thinking with reference to God as Creator, human beings as creatures, and the involvement of all of creation in the drama of the relationship between God and humans. "Nature, man, and God" is manifestly not the order of Paul's thinking.[22] Paul saw God, humans, and nature as closely related by original creation, by maintenance of creation, by cosmic redemption, and by future hope. All of this is united in Christ, the agent of creation, the Lord of the universe, the Redeemer, and the one with whom believers and the creation will be glorified.

These chapters on preaching and creation in Romans have set the stage for our survey of Paul's gospel logic beginning with sin and ending with Christian living.

> "The heavens declare the glory of God.... to him be glory in the church and in Christ Jesus throughout all generations, for ever and ever! Amen" (Ps. 19:1; Eph. 3:21).

For Further Reading

Brunner, Emil. *The Christian Doctrine of Creation and Redemption.* Philadelphia: The Westminster Press, 1952.

Gibbs, John G. *Creation and Redemption: A Study in Pauline Theology.* Leiden, Netherlands: E. J. Brill, 1971.

Reumann, John. *Creation & New Creation: The Past, Present, and Future of God's Creative Activity.* Minneapolis: Augsburg, 1973.

Schmitz-Moormann, Karl. *Theology of Creation in an Evolutionary World.* Cleveland: The Pilgrim Press, 1997.

Shields, Bruce E. *Creation in Romans.* Unpublished Dissertation, 1979.

Young, Norman. *Creator, Creation and Faith.* London: William Collins Sons & Co. Ltd., 1976.

CHAPTER 3

What Romans Says about Sin

Paul wastes no time getting to the discomforting topic of sin. First, he states his intention to lay out for the Roman believers the gospel of Christ. Immediately, he shows that God's righteousness is revealed in the gospel. As soon as he has laid that basic foundation, he turns to the first aspect of that revelation: the revelation of the wrath of God on the wickedness of the human race. Romans 1:18–32 is one of the most graphic descriptions in all of scripture of what we usually refer to as sin. Yet Paul indicates that *what we usually call sin* is but *a symptom,* or even *a result of the actual primary sin.*

> For the wrath of God is revealed from heaven against all ungodliness and wickedness of those who by their wickedness suppress the truth. For what can be known about God is plain to them, because God has shown it to them. Ever since the creation of the world his eternal power and divine nature, invisible though they are, have been understood and seen through the things he has made. So they are without excuse; for though they knew God, they did not honor him as God or give thanks to him, but they became futile in their thinking, and their senseless minds were darkened. Claiming to be wise, they became fools; and they exchanged the glory of the immortal God for images resembling a mortal human being or birds or four-footed animals or reptiles.

Therefore God gave them up in the lusts of their hearts to impurity, to the degrading of their bodies among themselves, because they exchanged the truth about God for a lie and worshiped and served the creature rather than the Creator, who is blessed forever! Amen.

For this reason God gave them up to degrading passions. Their women exchanged natural intercourse for unnatural, and in the same way also the men, giving up natural intercourse with women, were consumed with passion for one another. Men committed shameless acts with men and received in their own persons the due penalty for their error.

And since they did not see fit to acknowledge God, God gave them up to a debased mind and to things that should not be done. They were filled with every kind of wickedness, evil, covetousness, malice. Full of envy, murder, strife, deceit, craftiness, they are gossips, slanderers, God-haters, insolent, haughty, boastful, inventors of evil, rebellious toward parents, foolish, faithless, heartless, ruthless. They know God's decree, that those who practice such things deserve to die—yet they not only do them but even applaud others who practice them.

The first step in presenting the gospel is to convince the hearer that he or she needs it. Paul begins his exposition of the gospel of salvation by looking at the wrath of God and the sin of humans that calls forth that wrath. God's wrath is not arbitrary as seemed to be the case with the chief Roman god, Jupiter, god of the storm. The wrath Paul points to is occasioned by the sinful lives of human beings. It is revealed "against all ungodliness and wickedness of those who by their wickedness suppress the truth" (v. 18). Just what he means by this he explains in the next several verses. First, he points out that they (humans in general, or at least all Gentiles) should have known about the true God since God has made it possible for everybody to know something about God. What can be known? God's "eternal power and divine nature" (v. 19). How can this be known? God can be "understood and seen through the things he has made" (v. 20). This reads literally "by the works," a statement that, similar to Psalm 103:22, sees God's works in creation as speaking. This is not idle speculation, not what some would call natural theology. The reason Paul begins with a revelation of God available to everybody is to point out that everybody is "without excuse." Nobody can plead innocence. We all experience the creation in which we live, and this should stimulate us to seek its Creator.

Verses 21–23 define humanity's basic sin, as Paul viewed it: idolatry. This act of rebellion begins negatively: "they did not honor him as God or give thanks to him" (v. 21). This refusal to worship the true God leads to a futility of thinking and to a darkening of the heart. Thus, both reason and will are damaged. This lays the foundation for the peculiar conflict between the concept of wisdom common to sinful human beings and the true divine wisdom that shows our brand to be foolish.

Paul develops this contrast further in 1 Corinthians 1 and 2. The final step in this process of sin is the actual development of idol worship. As Bob Dylan wrote, you've "Gotta Serve Somebody."[1] People do not go around consciously seeking an object of worship. We simply cannot be objective and detached about everything around us. If we refuse to glorify the Creator, we seem bound to exchange the glory of the immortal God for images of something around us. Worship is not bad; in fact, it is inescapable. But to worship anything or any person other than God is to focus on something secondary instead of primary, something finite instead of infinite, something made instead of its Maker. This accords ultimate status to something less than ultimate, which misses the mark completely.

The rest of the chapter reads like a catalog of sins; but if we catch the import of the refrain, "God gave them up" (vv. 24, 26, 28), we see that the basic sin is still idolatry, as Paul reiterates in verse 25. The rest of the transgressions are listed as punishments for sin or at least results of sin. It is hardly necessary to comment on the details here. Our English versions translate Paul's lists graphically enough for us to recognize what he is saying. Sexual immorality and murder are listed alongside greed, gossip, and disobedience of parents, with no distinction noted. All these acts and attitudes are seen as unnatural. They go against the will of God, that will by which we humans and the universe in which we live are created. And the whole mess is traceable to our rebellious refusal to glorify God as Creator.

As we read chapter 2, Paul narrows his focus somewhat. Romans 1:18–32 shows sin to be in the background and experience of all of us, but some people are always ready to "judge others" (2:1). In 2:1–11, Paul turns the gospel's spotlight on these people. If only one basic sin exists and if everybody is doing it, then all sin's symptoms—all of what we call sins—are equally damaging. They show that the perpetrator is out of touch with God. Thus Paul has good reason to remind people that "in passing judgment on another you condemn yourself, because you, the judge, are doing the very same things" (2:1*b*).

The apostle's main concern is not so much the social or psychological results of the sin of judging. He goes right to the heart of the matter. He warns that such an attitude puts persons in danger of God's judgment. Here we learn God occupies the judge's role; we do not. The person judging others is playing God, who "shows no partiality" (2:11).

In verses 12 and 13, Paul reverts to the law and indicates that the person who actually keeps the law is justified by it. However, Paul has already indicated and will soon make clearer that nobody keeps either the written law or the law written on the heart (2:14–15).

With 2:17, Paul turns unambiguously to his own people, the Jews. He first describes what being a Jew means and then accuses the Jews of living in such a way that they bring dishonor to the very God they claim to have a special relationship with. So, even Jews at their best are sinners in need of forgiveness.

The rest of this chapter and the beginning of chapter 3 deal with some of Paul's personal concerns about the place of the Jews in the plan of God and about the relationship between the righteous God and the sin of humanity. Paul caps this section with a chain of quotations from the Hebrew Scriptures, all of which lament the total sinfulness of humanity. Then in 3:23, Paul summarizes his whole exposition of sin with the familiar words, "all have sinned and fall short of the glory of God."

This linking sin with the glory of God is fascinating. The term translated "fall short" could just as well be rendered "lack." In Jewish thinking, the glory of God was not just a characteristic of the divinity. The glory of God was a quality Adam and Eve originally possessed. They lost it as a result of sin. In the first-century Jewish document *The Life of Adam and Eve,*[2] we read that Eve, after having eaten of the forbidden fruit, said to the serpent, "Why have you done this to me, that I have been estranged from my glory with which I was clothed?" This narrative continues with Adam's fall and his statement to Eve, which ends, "You have estranged me from the glory of God." Paul and his Jewish contemporaries, among whom were some of the Roman Christians, understood lacking the glory of God as a direct result of sin from the time of Adam and Eve and their initial act of rebellion. Paul apparently taught that sin attacks the essence of our created nature.

Paul comes back to deal with sin in chapters 5, 6, and 7, but these first three chapters lay the groundwork for his doctrine of sin. In 5:12–21, he shows Adam, indeed, brought sin into the world by sinning, that is, by disobeying God. In chapter 6, Paul proclaims that God frees Christians from sin; therefore, Christians should no longer put themselves under sin's control. Chapter 7 describes, in a personal way, that sin gets its foothold in the human life because we try to be righteous under our own power. This leaves us in despair. Stirring news follows in the opening verses of chapter 8. God has done what could be accomplished in no other way, including through the law. In Christ, God has condemned sin in the flesh and disarmed all real condemnation of those who receive justification through faith.

Just as the gospel is a power, Paul sees sin as a power, one closely related to death and empowered by the combination of the law's demands and the weakness of human flesh. Since sin is a power that can control human beings, only God can deal ultimately with it. He has done that through the power of the gospel, a power that can free us from sin and keep us free and safe.

For Further Reading

See commentaries on Romans 1:18–2:29 and works on the law and ethics listed at the end of chapters 4 and 7.

CHAPTER 4

What Romans Says about Justification/Righteousness

The English words *justification* and *righteousness* are translations of one word in Greek: *dikaiosyne.* When *dikaiosyne* appears as a noun, the word *righteousness* is often an adequate equivalent. The problem is that English has no verb form for righteousness. In Greek the verb form is most often used to describe a judge declaring an accused person innocent (righteous). The closest equivalent we have is *justify* and its noun form *justification. Justification* refers to the act of declaring a person righteous.

The term is further complicated in Romans and elsewhere by its reference not only to humans but also to God. Paul asserts that in the gospel "the righteousness of God is revealed" (1:17). In the Hebrew scriptures, God's righteousness (Hebrew *tsedek*), as well as God's holiness, points to God's integrity, God's being true to God's self as well as to the covenant between God and mortals. Righteousness is a primary characteristic of God. The Israelites often called upon God's own righteousness to relieve them of some enemy or to overcome a difficult circumstance in spite of their own unrighteousness, e.g., Isa. 51; Ps. 143. They expected God's righteousness would put things right in the end times (see e.g., Pss. 96; 98). This became a major theme in the Dead Sea Scrolls and the intertestamental literature.

However, *righteousness* is also used in these places to refer to human beings. People can be righteous if they live up to the demands of God's law. Of course, Paul contends that nobody does that. Thus nobody is righteous before God, the righteous judge, whose act of justification makes people righteous. Paul has plenty of scripture to support him as he shows by the texts he quotes in Romans 3:10–18. This chain includes passages from Psalms, Ecclesiastes, and Proverbs.

The verb form of *dikaiosyne* enters here. One form or another of this root appears seven times in 3:21–26:

> But now, apart from law, the righteousness [*dikaiosyne*] of God has been disclosed, and is attested by the law and the prophets, the righteousness [*dikaiosyne*] of God through faith in Jesus Christ for all who believe. For there is no distinction, since all have sinned and fall short of the glory of God; they are now justified [*dikaioumenoi*] by his grace as a gift, through the redemption that is in Christ Jesus, whom God put forward as a sacrifice of atonement by his blood, effective through faith. He did this to show his righteousness [*dikaiosyne*], because in his divine forbearance he had passed over the sins previously committed; it was to prove at the present time that he himself is righteous [*dikaion*] and that he justifies [*dikaiounta*] the one who has faith in Jesus.

The NRSV committee decided not to translate one use of *dikaiosyne* in verse 26 probably because it would seem redundant. But redundancy is one means Paul uses to make a point. By means of the death of Jesus, God is able to declare righteous those who are unrighteous and at the same time guard the divine righteousness.

Verse 24 states that the righteousness Paul discusses here is not the virtuous life of the human being. Rather, it is the gift God gives to the person who receives it in faith. This is the way God deals with the mess human beings created by their sinning.

Paul's term grace (*charis*) enters the discussion. This is such a typical term for Paul—and so central to his thought—that he habitually uses it as a greeting in place of the normal Greek *chairein* (compare Rom. 1:7 with Jas. 1:1). He usually links it with *eirene,* the Greek equivalent of the Hebrew *shalom. Shalom* has a broad meaning akin to our "salvation." This is a radical departure from the normal use of the term by Jews or Greeks. This grace is a concept that we preachers have trouble getting across to people. In America, we have been conditioned to emulate people who depend on no one else and who create and control their own lives.[1] Preachers find it difficult to convince Americans they need someone else's grace, even when that someone is God.

This new view of goodness as a gift instead of an accomplishment makes sense only in gospel logic. This logic assumes the universality of sin and its effects on all humans. Paul appears to have had trouble communicating this in his day also, since he returns to the theme often in his epistles and uses the most radical metaphors possible to show the contrast between one's pre-Christian state and the condition of the believer. Paul knows what grace does. It changes us from enemies to children, from slaves to free people, from death to life. In other words, grace changes us from outsiders to insiders. Grace reveals itself because God wants us inside so much that the death of the Son of God was not too much to pay.

For Paul (as we shall see in chapter 11), justification is the umbrella term for the experience of becoming and remaining a Christian. However, he used many other terms from various areas of human experience. Becoming righteous means a radical change in every aspect of life. This is not just a religious term. For Paul, becoming righteous was not especially religious at all. It was more ethical and forensic. The picture one gets in his use of *dikaiosyne* is that of a courtroom where we mortals stand before God the Judge. Instead of declaring us unrighteous, as we deserve, God declares us righteous. Paul did not see this as funny celestial bookkeeping. God does not play games of "let's pretend." In Paul's picture, God's word is the power that brought forth the whole universe, so God's declaration of righteousness creates righteous people from the unlikely raw material of sinful humans.

Here in Romans 3, Paul begins using his extensive glossary of salvation terms. In verses 24 and 25, he links justification with redemption and atonement. Redemption is another term with deep significance for Israel. It comes from the domain of business, specifically the business of slavery. One can redeem another from slavery by paying the price for that person's freedom. People who got into deep debt sometimes had to sell themselves into slavery to get the money they needed to pay off their debts. This put them in position to need relatives or close friends to redeem them from debt slavery. As a nation, Israel understood its time in Egypt as slavery from which God had redeemed them. Therefore, in Paul's mind, history had already linked the righteousness of God with God's acting on behalf of his people to redeem or free them from slavery. Chapter 6 discusses salvation as being freed from slavery to sin (vv. 15–23).

This redemption, Paul asserts, is "in Christ Jesus, whom God put forward as a sacrifice of atonement by his blood, effective through faith." The term translated "sacrifice of atonement" refers to the "mercy seat," the golden shelf above the ark of the covenant in the Jerusalem temple. There, on the Day of Atonement, the high priest took the blood of sacrifice for the sins of the people to present it to God. Paul concluded that the blood of the sacrifice is Christ's. Christ is the symbol of God's presence to receive the sacrifice. In this way, Christ's death becomes the means of God's forgiveness of sins. Paul even more clearly connects justification and forgiveness in 4:1–8 (see chapter 10).

In 5:1–11, Paul introduces more of his glossary: peace, access to grace, hope of glory, salvation, and reconciliation. Justification is the first and primary metaphor Paul uses for what we call salvation–this right relationship with God made possible through Jesus Christ's faithfulness. Paul draws from different semantic domains, showing that the gospel is not just another religious doctrine or philosophical concept. It affects every aspect of our lives in a radical way and effects a new creation.

Paul assembles what might be the basic before and after contrast in Romans 4. Romans 4:5 reads: "But to one who without works trusts him who justifies the ungodly, such faith is reckoned as righteousness." God justifies the ungodly (*asebe*), one of the words Paul uses in Romans 1:18 to describe those against whom the wrath of God is revealed. That is as bluntly as one could describe what Paul means by *dikaiosyne*. Instead of sending us the wrath of the heavenly Judge, God declares us righteous. Paul calls this same God as "the God in whom he [Abraham] believed, who gives life to the dead and calls into existence the things that do not exist" (4:17). God the justifier is, thus, God the Creator.

Paul closes the chapter by referring to "him who raised Jesus our Lord from the dead, who was handed over to death for our trespasses and was raised for our justification" (4:24b-25). Justification is equivalent to new creation, as is shown in the resurrection of Christ. This harmonizes nicely with 2 Corinthians 5:17 and Galatians 6:15, where Paul uses the explicit term, "new creation." The ultimate contrast in regard to justification for Paul, then, is that once we were nothing and now we are new creations, fit for service in God's reign and children in God's family.

Paul's teaching on justification and righteousness challenges the contemporary preacher to find in our cultures the terms that point to the totality of this Christian experience. Paul draws from many different human experiences, and we should, too. Some of Paul's terms can still work if we can say them without sounding too theological. We need to explain and illustrate these important concepts as metaphors from real life instead of ecclesiastical jargon. Let's not just echo Paul; let's emulate him.

For Further Reading

Boers, Hendrikus. *The Justification of the Gentiles.* Peabody, Mass.: Hendrickson, 1994.

Carson, D. A., Peter T. O'Brien, and Mark A. Seifrid, eds. *Justification and Variegated Nomism: A Fresh Appraisal of Paul and Second Temple Judaism.* Grand Rapids: Baker Academic, 2001.

Grieb, A. Katherine. *The Story of Romans: A Narrative Defense of God's Righteousness.* Louisville: Westminster John Knox Press, 2002.

Interpretation 57/1 (January 2003).

Martin, Ralph P. *Reconciliation: A Study of Paul's Theology.* Atlanta: John Knox Press, 1981.

Oden, Thomas C. *The Justification Reader.* Grand Rapids: W. B. Eerdmans, 2002.

Piper, John. *The Justification of God.* Grand Rapids: Baker Book House, 1983.

Reumann, John H. P. *Righteousness in the New Testament: Justification in the United States Lutheran-Roman Catholic Dialogue.* Philadelphia: Fortress Press, 1982.

Scroggs, Robin. *The Last Adam.* Philadelphia: Fortress Press, 1966.

Stuhlmacher, Peter. *Revisiting Paul's Doctrine of Justification: A Challenge to the New Perspective.* Downers Grove, Ill.: InterVarsity Press, 2001.

CHAPTER 5

What Romans Says about Eschatology

Interest in the end times has come and gone many times in the history of Judaism and Christianity. As I write this (August, 2002), it seems to be at high tide again. Books of both serious scholarship and fiction are proliferating, One of the fictionalized volumes on the rapture and tribulation just topped *The New York Times* best-sellers list the first week of its publication. So what does Paul have to say in Romans about the end times?

We might best see Paul's approach by looking at the various ways he uses the term "glory" (*doxa*). The noun *doxa* appears sixteen times in Romans, scattered evenly throughout the letter. The verb form *doxazo* appears five times. The original meaning of the Greek root is reputation or opinion, but this meaning changed between the time of Homer and Herodotus and the time of the early Christian writers.[1]

Paul uses the word in a rather strange way in several Romans passages. The first appearance (1:23) points to a reality about God's nature, which humans exchanged for something less. Then 3:23 states: "all have sinned and fall short of the glory of God." Here *doxa* appears to be something (or a condition) of which one falls short when one sins. In 5:2, Paul states that as a result of our justification in Christ, "we boast in our hope of sharing the glory of God." *Doxa* is something to hope for, but it is the means (power?) of Jesus' resurrection in

54

6:4. The most blatantly eschatological passage in Romans (8:18, 21) uses *doxa* as something hoped for that will affect not only humankind, but also the whole creation. This is enough to show that we are dealing with a concept bigger than reputation or honor. It has anthropological, cosmological, soteriological, and eschatological significance.

The Glory That Was

The meaning of the word *doxa,* in the New Testament is largely dependent on its equivalent in the Hebrew Bible. The Septuagint translators decided to use *doxa* to translate the Hebrew *kabod.*[2] They filled this rather superficial Greek word with deep cultic and theological significance, especially for the Jews.[3] It retained the meaning of reputation or honor, but it went much deeper than that, for *kabod* denotes appearance in the sense of that which reveals the real nature.[4]

Isaiah uses it in 35:2 to refer to the appearance of beauty in the creation and metaphorically in 17:4 to refer to the appearance of Jacob. More important, Isaiah 48:11 indicates that God's glory is the divine authority and power among God's people, and Psalms 96 and 97 treat *kabod* as the whole being and power of God. Perhaps most decisive are Exodus 24:15–17 and 40:34–35, where the glory of God is a reality—nearly a substance—which one could call God's presence on the mountain or in the tabernacle. Thus, God's glory comes to be understood as almost identical with God's nature or person, at least as far as it is possible for humans to understand it or respond to it.[5]

The further anthropological development of the meaning of *doxa* came about in the schools of rabbinical thinking within Palestinian Judaism. The rabbis identified the glory of God with the image of God, in which Adam and Eve were created. The original humans shared God's glory. This is illustrated by a number of fantastic legends describing Adam as a huge figure with divine powers. As we saw in chapter 3, this glory was thought to have been withdrawn as a result of sin, as is most clearly stated in the *Apocalypse of Moses* 20 and 21. There Eve, after having eaten of the fruit, says to the serpent: "Why hast thou done this to me in that thou hast deprived me of the glory with which I was clothed?" Adam, after his eating, cries out: "O wicked woman! What have I done to thee that thou hast deprived me of the glory of God?"[6]

That Paul accepted this full understanding of the meaning of *doxa* should be clear. In Romans 5 he spells out the implications of the sin of Adam and of the reconciliation offered in Christ, whom he calls the one Man. He makes this same contrast in 1 Corinthians 15:21–28. In this light, the construction of Romans 5 is interesting. Verse 2 has us boasting in hope of God's glory; then verse 3 states that we exult in our tribulations, and verse 11 has us exulting in God through our Lord Jesus Christ. This introduces the Adam-Christ typology in verses 12–21.

If this is not enough to convince us of Paul's broad understanding of *doxa*, 1 Corinthians 15:40–49 should complete the case. Here we find him using *doxa* with sun, moon, stars, and human bodies. If *appearance* or *nature* is substituted for glory, the sense remains the same. Verse 45 returns to the Adam-Christ contrast, calling Christ the "last Adam," then contrasting the natural (*psychikon*) with the spiritual (*pneumatikon*), the earthly with the heavenly. Verse 49 promises, "just as we have borne the image of the earthly, we shall also bear the image of the heavenly." Here we have image, Adam, spirit, and glory all in relation to the whole of creation and all in a context suspended between the resurrection of Christ and the parousia. The same themes are related in the same ways in Romans, where an understanding of the full meaning of *doxa* is vital to its interpretation.

We should recognize that in many cases *doxa* retains its original meaning of honor. But nine appearances in Romans clearly mean more than this. The sin of idolatry exchanges the "glory of the immortal God for images resembling a mortal human being or birds" (1:23). Romans 3:23 echoes the *Apocalypse of Moses*[7] when it states: "all have sinned and fall short of [or lack] the glory of God." In 6:4, "the glory of the Father" is the means of Christ's resurrection. Both appearances in chapter 8 are eschatological. Verse 18 compares today's sufferings with "the glory about to be revealed," and verse 21 promises that the creation itself will "obtain the freedom of the glory of the children of God." The three appearances in 9:4 and 23 continue this same image, rooted in the Hebrew scriptures and developed by the rabbis and the apocalyptists.[8]

Doxa is for Paul—when he uses it in this cosmic sense—the nature that God intended for the creation. In the case of humankind, that glory was forfeited as a result of disobedience. This loss threw the whole of creation out of balance in addition to permitting humans to be subject to their fleshly impulses instead of controlling them.

However, in the person of Christ Jesus, the alienation of human beings from the glory of God and the resultant process of increasing slavery to sin were reversed. As a result of his death and resurrection (by means of God's glory), the possibility of restoration to the status of original creation is offered to all. This offer promises a limited foretaste here and now with perfect restoration in the future. Christ has made it possible, the Spirit makes it real, and God promises the future perfection. The glorification of Christ means "the world's recovering the character of creation."[9]

With this promise of glorification, Paul reaches back to original creation, deals with the reality of new creation, and looks forward to the restoration of God's purpose in creation—a restoration whose fulfillment awaits the eschaton.

The Glory That Will Be, Romans 8:18–30

To speak about glorification, Paul has to defend his hope against the reality of present sufferings. This seeming contradiction must have been a constant challenge to early Christian apologists. First Peter 4:12–5:1 (and 5:10) deals with the same question in reference to *doxa.* Just how does Paul deal with it? Romans 8:18–30 forms a well-organized and tightly reasoned unity with the proposition (v. 18), three warrants (vv. 19–22, 23–25, and 26–27), and a conclusion (28–30). For each of the warrants, Paul offers a supporting statement and an implication.

Warrant 1

Paul uses the witness of the creation as the first warrant for his persuasion that the present sufferings do not compare with the coming glory. It must be significant that he uses his central concept of *doxa* in the contrast. *Doxa* does not appear often, but it seems vital each time it does appear.

The syntax of verses 19–22 is rather straightforward. Verse 19 states the claim that Paul presents as evidence for his hope. It is joined directly to verse 18 with the conjunction *gar* (for). The subject is "the earnest expectation of the creation" (note that NRSV makes creation the subject). This "expectation" is awaiting the revelation of God's children. Paul establishes this claim with a statement about the past and one about the future of creation. Verse 20 states that the creation was subjected to futility (or perhaps better, frustration: *mataioteti*), not willingly, but by the one who subjected it on the basis of hope. Hope is again the connecting link since verse 21 defines something of the content of this hope: The creation will be freed from the slavery to mortality to the freedom of the *doxa* of the children of God. Verse 22 states the present result of this expectation: The whole creation groans and travails together until this moment.

I see verse 21 as Paul's clearest eschatological statement in Romans, but its clarity comes from an accurate understanding of *doxa*. This glory is more than a feeling of victory; it is a restoration of the Creator's intent for the human race. The glory in which mortals were created was lost as a result of sin. Then Christ came. In his act of forgiveness, he gave us a hope of glory. Thus in 8:21 with the whole of creation, Paul looks forward to the "freedom of the glory of the children of God" (*eis ten eleutherian tes doxes ton teknon tou theou*). This string of three genitives is often translated as though *doxa* were an adjective ("the glorious freedom of the children of God," NIV). However, in our understanding of Paul's use of *doxa*, this sentence points to the restoration of the originally created glory of the human race. This means freedom from sin, death, and the ungodly activities of life under the dominion of sin. As restored children of God, our eternal life with God will be more than life stretching forward without end. It will be life as God intended–life for which we have yearned, without knowing what we were looking for. In other words, Paul's eschatological hope is that believers will be restored to a kind of life of which we have only faint racial memories–life as God created it.

The Glory That Is

Warrant 2

As mentioned earlier, Romans 5:2 assures the believer that we can boast, or rejoice, in the hope of God's glory on the basis of our justification in Christ. This is the present tense eschatology that Paul spells out in more detail at the end of chapter 8.

He has looked at the creation as evidence of the coming glory. Verse 23 summarizes that warrant ("and not only the creation") and turns to believers as his second warrant ("but we ourselves who have the first fruits of the Spirit"). The creation is groaning in labor pains; likewise, we "groan inwardly while we wait for adoption, the redemption of our bodies." Paul has already assured Christians of their adoption as children of God (8:15–17) and of their redemption (3:24). That comprises the "already" nature of their relationship with God. Next, he explains that the full experience of this relationship is "not yet." Christians live in the eschatological time. God has won the victory, but the end of the conflict remains in the future.

8:24–25 continues this theme: "For in hope we were saved. Now hope that is seen is not hope. For who hopes for what is seen? But if we hope for what we do not see, we wait for it with patience."

Note the tenses here: *hope* is future oriented, but Paul mixes hope with the statement "we were saved" in the past tense. Salvation is a reality, but it is not yet fulfilled. The lack of fulfillment we experience in our sufferings and frustrations testifies to the glorification awaiting us in God's future. The present tense shows what is involved in this life of hope.

Warrant 3

Verses 26–27 assure the believer that the Holy Spirit helps us in the weakness of our prayer life. The creation groans in testimony to God's future. Our own groaning is Paul's second witness. Here is his third, the Holy Spirit. In verse 23, he describes Christians as people "who have the first fruits of the Spirit," another reality not fully actualized. Yet the example of the Spirit's presence is strangely comforting. In our frustration, when facing life's challenges, we often do not even know how to pray. Paul assures (or reminds) us the Spirit helps us even in this weakness, interceding for us. Therefore, we can be assured that God understands, "because the Spirit intercedes for the saints according to the will of God."

Conclusion

Paul sums up his argument for "the glory about to be revealed to us." Verses 28–30 indicate that we have been in God's plan from the beginning. Terms like "foreknew" and "predestined" have spawned theological debates throughout the centuries of Christian history. However, debating over precise definitions misses Paul's point, namely, that God is ultimately in charge. God's purpose will be carried out one way or another, sooner or later. Those who love God and "who are called according to his purpose" are on the winning side—the company of those whom God "called" and "justified" and even "glorified."

The remainder of the chapter is a detailed assurance that nothing "will be able to separate us from the love of God in Christ Jesus our Lord." Verses 31–34 show that the only person who could possibly be our accuser is actually our defense attorney (see chapter 13). In verses 35–37, nothing this world can throw at us can separate us from God. Verses 37–39, in a flight of poetic beauty, proclaim that none of the metaphysical powers can accomplish such separation either.

The hope of glory is not just future oriented. This hope entails the present reality of Christ's intercession for us, as well as the present reality of our constant connection with God's love. This is all actualized in our lives by means of the Holy Spirit, whom we have as a down payment on the reality of eternal life in God's presence. So Paul's eschatology is never merely future. We are living in the eschaton, but it is not yet fully realized.

For Further Reading

Beker, J. Christiaan. *Paul's Apocalyptic Gospel.* Philadelphia: Fortress Press, 1982.

——. *The Triumph of God.* Minneapolis: Fortress Press, 1990.

Eastman, Susan. "Whose Apocalypse? The Identity of the Sons of God in Romans 8:19." *Journal of Biblical Literature* 121, no. 2 (Summer 2002): 263–77.

Johnson, E. Elizabeth. *The Function of Apocalyptic and Wisdom Traditions in Romans 9–11.* Atlanta: Scholars Press, 1989.

Longenecker, Bruce W. *Eschatology and the Covenant: A Comparison of 4 Ezra and Romans 1–11,* Journal for the Study of the New Testament Supplement Series 57. Sheffield, England: JSOT Press, 1991.

Vos, Geerhardus. *The Pauline Eschatology.* Grand Rapids: W. B. Eerdmans, 1972.

CHAPTER 6

What Romans Says about Law/*Torah*

Paul's understanding of and attitude toward the Mosaic law may be the most overworked or controversial issue in the study of the apostle. Saul of Tarsus had been a faithful adherent of the Jewish law. He described himself as "circumcised on the eighth day, a member of the people of Israel, of the tribe of Benjamin, a Hebrew born of Hebrews; as to the law, a Pharisee; as to zeal, a persecutor of the church; as to righteousness under the law, blameless" (Phil. 3:5–6).

One might wonder what it would take to turn that kind of zeal for *Torah* in another direction. Paul's experience on the road to Damascus was radical enough to begin the process, but we can only wish we had more information about his thought processes during the next fourteen years. He wrote to the Galatians (2:1) that it was only after fourteen years following his Damascus road experience[1] that he began his leadership ministry in Antioch. Judging from his writings in Romans and Galatians, he had thoroughly studied the *Torah*, this time in the light of his new understanding that Jesus of Nazareth was the Messiah.

He appears to have concluded that the *Torah* is a valid word from God, that it reveals God's will for the covenant people and to some extent for the whole human race, and that it continues to be "holy and just and good" (Rom. 7:12). At the same time, he sees that the *Torah* is not a means of human justification before God. He recognizes that the Hebrew Scriptures teach that God's gracious choice called Israel into a covenant relationship with their Lord. The law was given to them as a gift of that grace. This divine grace, he discovered, is most clearly and attractively demonstrated in the faithful death of Jesus and his resurrection from the dead. Thus, he could conclude in Romans 10:4, "Christ is the end of the law so that there may be righteousness for everyone who believes."

Two aspects of this sentence are difficult to interpret. The first is the meaning of "end." The Greek word *telos* carries the implication of end in the sense of fulfillment the intended end. The second is the last phrase, which the NRSV translates, "so that there may be righteousness for everyone who believes." The original here is *eis dikaiosyne panti to pisteuonti*–literally "unto righteousness (or justification) to all who believe." I believe Paul meant that if justification had ever come through the *Torah,* that justification came to a halt in Christ.

This does not mean that Christ's coming abrogated the law. Paul did not stand in tension with Christ's relation to the law and the Sermon on the Mount statement, "I have come not to abolish but to fulfill [the law]" (Mt. 5:17b). The terminology is different, but the thrust is the same. As Paul put it in Romans 8:3, "For God has done what the law, weakened by human flesh, could not do: by sending his own Son in the likeness of sinful flesh, and to deal with sin, he condemned sin in the flesh."

How, then, is the *Torah* related to sin? Paul points out that Adam's sin was disobedience of God's command (Rom. 5:12–21). So Adam stands for the human who disobeys. Christ is the exemplar of the obedient person. The results of Christ's obedience are more powerful and far-reaching than the results of Adam's disobedience. At the base of this contrast lies the understanding that sin is disobedience of the Lord. In other words, sin is the breaking of a law or disregard for the Lord's instruction.

This leads us to Paul's personal dealing with sin and the law in Romans 7. The chapter begins (vv. 1–6) with an illustration from the laws concerning marriage. From this Paul concludes that in our connection with the death of Christ (in baptism—see 6:3–11), we are freed from the law and are free to serve God. Verse 7 opens with the question, "What then should we say? That the law is sin?" (7:7) Paul responds with his characteristic strong negative retort (*me genoito*), explaining that the law (and here he got personal) has helped him to know the seriousness of sin and awakened in him an interest in, or even an attraction to, the sins the law describes and proscribes.

Verse 10 contains the negative statement, "the very commandment that promised life proved to be death to me." Verse 11 follows with an echo of Genesis 3:13. Eve replied to God's question about what she had done, "The serpent tricked me, and I ate." The Septuagint (LXX), the Greek translation, used a term (*epatesen*) related to the term Paul used in Romans 7:11, "For sin, seizing an opportunity in the commandment, deceived me (*exepatesen*) and through it killed me." The onus here is not on the law but on the power of sin and on the weakness of human flesh. Therefore, Paul follows that negativity with verse 12: "So the law is holy, and the commandment is holy and just and good." As negative as Paul could seem about the law, he always returns to this sort of praise of the law. He insists that its weakness really lies elsewhere. He would not dismiss the *Torah* as a mistake of God or a misunderstanding of Israel. He contends the combination of the law and human frailty was never strong enough to deal with sin as a power or as a human tendency.

When he gives directions for living the Christian life, he turns to the *Torah*. Romans 13:8–10 begins, "Owe no one anything except to love one another; for the one who loves another has fulfilled the law." Here the same word for fulfill appears as that used in the Sermon on the Mount statement. Paul quotes four of the Ten Commandments, seeing them "summed up in this word, 'Love your neighbor as yourself.'" We also find this Christian-sounding summary of the law in Galatians 5:14 and in Jesus' teaching in Mark 12:31 and its parallels. Paul does not simply take this from Jesus, however. Its roots are not New Testament, but Old as in Lev. 19:18. Paul sees no need to "reinvent the wheel," as we might say. He shows no signs of antinomianism, opposition to the law. He only desires to let the *Torah* apply where it was meant to apply, without making more demands on it than God intended for it.

Much of our difficulty with Paul and the law stems from the Protestant Reformation. The Reformers protested against the legalistic penance and sacramental systems of the medieval Roman Catholic Church. Martin Luther, and to a lesser extent John Calvin, reacted so strongly against any hint that human works could participate in the process of salvation that they (and their followers in Protestant orthodoxy) found it difficult to see Paul's positive statements about the law. This insight into the danger of hermeneutical blinders should make us doubly concerned to read carefully what the apostle wrote and to reserve our conclusions until we see the whole argument.

Even as late as the writing of Romans, Paul maintained a deep reverence for the *Torah* and for its importance in instructing mortals in the Creator's intentions for the human race. Paul carefully reminds us that the law is not intended to make one race superior to others or to give anybody a way to earn God's favor. He insists rather that we are equally sinners, whether our transgression is against the *Torah* or against our own consciences and reading of creation. God's favor comes to all as a gift accessible by faith.

Paul loved the law and saw it as the *paidagogos hemon gegonen eis Christon* (our disciplinarian leading us to Christ, Gal. 3:24). Scholars and preachers have often misunderstood, mistranslated, and misapplied this verse. The *paidagogos* was the household slave with the responsibility to keep the children safe and in order. This slave delivered the master's children to the teacher and retrieved them back home. The picture is clear. Paul saw that the law's primary purpose was to prepare the human race for the coming of Christ, in whom we would all find our justification by faith. Along with the other positive statements about the law, this one is high praise since it makes the law inferior only to the ultimate divine revelation and salvation in Jesus Christ.

Paul may be saying the law is a helpful guide to living in the will of God, as long as we do not demand more of it than God intended. It is not a way to earn God's favor. God already loves us. It is not a way to work toward justification. In the redemptive death and resurrection of Jesus Christ, God has already done all that is necessary for our justification. Finally, the law is not power for living. God offers that power in the presence of the Holy Spirit.

As we shall see in the next chapter, this approach to law in general and Torah in particular does not leave the Christian helpless in the attempt to live up to God's expectations. Paul points out many principles within the Hebrew Scriptures and especially in the life of Jesus and the nature of the gospel to help us to live by faith.

For Further Reading

Davies, W. D. *Paul and Rabbinic Judaism.* Philadelphia: Fortress Press, 1980.

Dunn, James D. G. *Jesus, Paul, and the Law.* Louisville: Westminster/John Knox Press, 1990.

Ellis, E. Earle. *Paul's Use of the Old Testament.* Grand Rapids: Baker Book House, 1957.

Sanders, E. P. *Paul, the Law, and the Jewish People.* Philadelphia: Fortress Press, 1985.

——. *Paul and Palestinian Judaism.* Philadelphia: Fortress Press, 1977.

Schoeps, H. J. *Paul: The Theology of the Apostle in the Light of Jewish Religious History.* Philadelphia: The Westminster Press, 1961.

CHAPTER 7

What Romans Says about Ethics

Earlier chapters dealing with sin and justification have raised many ethical issues. Here, I will not pretend to offer a full survey of Paul's ethics, even in Romans. I will, instead, focus on chapters 12 and 13, where Paul offers both concrete advice and general principles for Christian living, and I will comment briefly on other passages that spread light on this one. The next chapter will deal with personal relationships as found in Romans 14–15.

As we noted in Chapter 3, Paul understands basic sin to be willful rebellion against God as Creator (Rom. 1–3). The acts we so often label as sins are the results of God's giving the rebels up (or over) to practices contrary to creation.[1] Each encounter with issues of sinful behavior in Paul reminds us that we live in a fallen world. We also see quickly that God has in Christ done something to remedy the situation.

The beautifully phrased Romans 12:1–2 turns Paul's discussion from more theologically oriented issues to Christian behavior. He sets the specific foundation of his ethics in Romans. He reminds the Roman Christians in many ways that their being Christians resulted from God's sacrificial act in the obedient death of Jesus Christ. God unleashed divine power to accompany that sacrifice by raising Jesus from the dead. The digest of that exposition is in 4:25: "[He] was handed over to death for our trespasses and was raised for our justification." In 12:1, Paul calls those who have been justified by that demonstration of God's mercies to make a general sacrifice. They should offer their bodies as that sacrifice—one that is living, holy, and acceptable to God. Such embodied sacrifice constitutes the Christians' peculiar brand of spiritual worship. Verse 2 teaches us that this kind of worship should result not in conformity to anything in the present aeon. Rather, it should transform us by renewing our minds. The result of this renewal is the discerning and documenting of "the will of God—what is good and acceptable and perfect."[2]

From that pad Paul launches a series of ethical statements. He deals with the church and continues on to proverb-style pieces of advice through the rest of chapter 12. Chapter 13 changes the pattern again by dwelling somewhat on relations to authority figures and general comments on love as the fulfillment of the law. This leads to a closing exhortation to right living.

What was Paul presenting in these chapters? Since he rejected law as a means of righteousness in the practice of fallen humans, it is unlikely that he means to give a series of rules and regulations here. Reading anything Paul wrote as law is ironic since he so often rejected such readings. I suggest we read him as offering examples of how the transformed life should look. An "*inclusio*" frames this section of the epistle in 12:1–2 and 13:14. Paul closes his argument for transformed living with the reminder that we are living in the eschatological age. We are tasting salvation and expecting its fulfillment (13:11–12*a*). This leads to the exhortation to live as in the day, not in the night (13:12*b*-13). Such light and darkness contrasts are among Paul's favorite rhetorical touches. Finally (v. 14), he encourages, "Instead, put on the Lord Jesus Christ, and make no provision for the flesh, to gratify its desires." To sacrifice oneself in response to the sacrificial mercy of God and to clothe oneself with the Lord Jesus Christ form the beginning and the end of Paul's ethic. The rest is the application of the Christian's determination to live appropriately.

Paul begins his series of examples of Christian living with the issue that our contemporary educators and counselors call "self-concept." How we think of ourselves determines to a great extent how we treat others. People in our "aeon" seem to be concerned about building positive self-esteem in children. Paul apparently did the opposite: "I say to everyone among you not to think of yourself more highly than you ought to think." Paul did not want to destroy anybody's self-esteem. He merely pointed out the implication of our living in the grace of God. He continued, "but to think with sober judgment, each according to the measure of faith that God has assigned." Paul knew of no measure of human worth that should supplant the work of God in us. In the next chapter, we shall examine how Paul in Romans 14 repeatedly reminds people how precious Christians are in God's sight and, therefore, how Christians should view one another as precious. We are works of God, people for whom Christ died. That is high self-worth indeed. However, that gives us no license to lord it over others. It merely makes all humans equal—equally needy and equally valued in God's plan.

In gospel logic, this brings us to consider the nature of the church as a society of justified sinners. Paul turns to the body metaphor as he does in other contexts (See 1 Cor. 6:15; 12:12–31). He focuses on our being members of one another (v. 5). No member is more important than another. Indeed, if the body is to function as intended, all members are necessary. Therefore, God has given each of us different abilities. Paul lists examples of these gifts, including some that everybody can practice (cheerfulness).

This list should erase any thought that Paul ever pushes for low self-esteem. He claims everybody has a place within and abilities to offer to the body. The problem we encounter most often in our churches is not high self-esteem, but just the opposite. In most churches I have known, few members have taken the new creation seriously. They see themselves as sinners with little worth and no abilities to offer. Here Paul insists that God has given the church the ability to carry out the divine will in our communities. We should respect the gifts all other members bring to that body and should gladly put them to work in the church.

Being familiar with 1 Corinthians 12–14, we should not be surprised that Paul follows a discussion of God's gifts to God's people with a reference to love:

> Let love be genuine; hate what is evil, hold fast to what
> is good; love one another with mutual affection; outdo
> one another in showing honor. Do not lag in zeal, be
> ardent in spirit, serve the Lord. Rejoice in hope, be
> patient in suffering, persevere in prayer. Contribute to
> the needs of the saints; extend hospitality to strangers.
> (Rom. 12:9–13)

This begins a list of exhortations in short format, similar to
the proverbs in the Hebrew Bible and elsewhere. Most of these
exhortations could fit on a bumper sticker or a T-shirt.
Commentators have tried to find a system in the list to outline
it, but without notable success. The statements in these five
verses seem to refer most directly to Christians in relation to
other Christians. Verse 14, however, turns without transition to
the Christian's relationship to enemies of the faith: "Bless those
who persecute you; bless and do not curse them." The rest of
the chapter switches from references to general conduct to a
final exhortation (vv. 17–21) about how to conduct oneself in
the situation of direct enmity.

If we look carefully at this section's rhetoric, we will see
how Paul intends this list to strike us. Having finished teaching
his readers what it means to be a Christian, he begins teaching
how a Christian is to live in the world.[3] Romans 12:1–2
introduces the whole section with the appeal to total dedication
to God. Verses 3–8 point to the reality of unity among God's
people and the gifts God gives us for living and serving. The
section concludes by dealing in some detail with specific
problems facing the believers in Rome (in chapters 13–15).
These include how to deal with the government and how to
solve disagreements among themselves.

Between these two major sections stands Romans 12:9–
21, a list of real challenges in the life of any Christian. The
challenges appear without any detail or instruction on how
to make decisions about them. Paul must have been offering
a number of bits of rather general advice to show the scope
of application of the dedicated life of the Christian. He
cannot address all issues in great detail, so he makes a
representative list and chooses two situations with which to

deal in some detail. He takes up the question of the authorities in 13:1–7 and returns to more general principles in the rest of chapter 13 before dealing with the problem of disunity in the church in 14:1–15:12.

This is not to say that these curt bits of advice are so general as to be of no help to us. On the contrary, when we face one of these situations, we should be able to follow the principles and the process of decision making given in these chapters. This should lead us to live the life the Bible so artfully and clearly portrays in this brief list of ethical exhortations. The admonitions in verses 11 and 12 are helpful guidance to the Christian in any age and in any circumstance. We are always in danger of losing our zeal. Most of us experience life as a constant struggle and want to feel as zealous or ardent as possible. The positive admonition is to keep our spiritual fervor. The original statement here describes one who is aglow or boiling with the Spirit. In order not to leave the impression that the Christian's zeal is a matter of emotion, Paul adds, "serve the Lord." Zeal is a matter of motivation, and the Holy Spirit is available to aid us in this regard. All motivation must lead to the nitty-gritty service that we present to the Lord by serving people who need it. Sometimes the special glow of the Spirit comes only after we have begun serving. That is to say, at times we must get to work even if we do not feel like it. Then we find the ardor returning.

To "rejoice in hope" we must have come to terms with living as Christians in the world. Although Christians should always look forward, they should also be able to find joy in their service in the world. Sometimes that service will bring "suffering," in which circumstance Paul exhorts us to be "patient." The kind of patience he refers to here involves endurance—the patience of the long distance runner. The secret to a Christian's ability to live such a life of victory is to "persevere in prayer." We dare not underestimate the importance of a disciplined life of prayer for the believer. Without communication with the Creator, we cannot expect the inner resources of the Spirit or the effectiveness in service that are otherwise available to us.

At the end of these rather specific exhortations, Paul makes another general statement, this one applying at least one aspect of being "transformed." Those who do not allow their environment to determine their lifestyle, but rather live as persons being transformed by Christ, will "not be overcome by evil, but overcome evil with good" (v. 21). If such a life were easy or automatic for the Christian, Paul would hardly have mentioned it. If it were impossible, he would not have exhorted us to do it. The Christian lifestyle is neither automatic nor impossible, but the person who wants to live at peace with everyone and who endures trying circumstances is going to shine like a light in the world, to the glory of God.

So far, Paul has depicted a community of Christians experiencing great power. Such people are totally dedicated to God. They have been transformed to do God's will instead of being molded by the age in which they live. They are noticeably different from their neighbors. They have their own kind of power. When such people are united in a community, their power can (and did) turn the world upside down. When Christians are so united, they can be described as "members of one another," and they will be able to live the kind of life Paul characterizes in 12:9–21. This is just the kind of community for which people long in an age of alienation such as ours. Such a light should not be hidden in a world of darkness.

For this reason it is important to consider the relationship of the Christian with the society at large. In Rome the government dominated society, so we should not be surprised that Paul next turns to the Christians' relationship with the authorities.

The exhortation in Romans 13:1–5 is rather clear. The identity of these earthly authorities has not been much of an issue until recently. Most students of the passage have assumed that Paul is referring to the political authorities, specifically the Roman government. This seems a safe enough assumption since the letter is addressed to "to all God's beloved in Rome" (1:7). However, Mark Nanos has suggested (argued, actually)[4] that this assumption accompanies the theory that the book of Romans shared the occasion of Galatians, that is, that Paul was in conflict with so-called Judaizers. But Nanos contends that Paul was writing to Christians living in close proximity to the Jewish community in Rome and that Paul was urging them to attend to the Noahide law as set out in the apostolic decree from the Jerusalem conference (Acts 15:23–29). Nanos argues that the authorities Paul had in mind were the Jewish synagogue authorities whom Paul characterizes in chapters 14 and 15 as the weaker brothers, those who had not yet accepted Jesus as Messiah.

I find Nanos's argument interesting and helpful, though not fully convincing. At the same time, I have long argued that Paul's use of the term *aeon* (12:2) should be understood to refer to anything in any human context that calls for the believer's loyalty or veneration. Therefore, Paul would be exhorting the Christians not to be conformed to the dictates of the Roman state or the claims of the Jewish religious leaders. He urges transformation, not conformation, to any person or system. So I continue to deal with the passage in terms of the civil government.

For Christians, Paul lists two motivational levels: fear (or common sense) and conscience (v. 5). Believers are like others in that we do not want to be jailed or otherwise penalized for infractions of the law. It makes sense to obey the law. Unlike unbelievers, however, we have a deeper motivation. We recognize the source of all authority to be in God, so we obey because of an inner compulsion. Paul states his fundamental premise in verse 1b: "there is no authority except from God." The logical next step follows: "and those authorities that exist have been instituted by God." The whole exhortation to good citizenship derives from this principle.[5] A Christian's conscience is more powerful than fear of punishment. This was illustrated dramatically later in the church's history. Christians were willing to die (often brutally) at the hands of their government rather than renounce their faith in Christ. Such decisions were being made even before the writing of the New Testament books was completed, as Revelation 13 shows.

Revelation 13 and Romans 13 are two extremely different kinds of literature, and the two characterize the political authorities in opposite ways. I need not discuss here the differences between Paul's discursive rhetoric and the apocalyptic style we encounter in Revelation. However, the second issue does deserve at least a cursory treatment. The time of writing of each of these texts is different. Paul wrote during the early years of Nero's reign as emperor when the *pax Romana* was the general reality of the Roman world. Christianity was not yet known as anything other than a sect of Judaism and was protected as a *religio licita* (a legal religion). On the other hand, Revelation appears to have been written late in that first century, when the Christians were being disowned by synagogue authorities and persecuted in various parts of the empire by both the society at large and the local authorities. So Paul could expect the authorities to reward good works, while the seer had to warn believers against the beastly authoritarian structures of the later generation.

However, these two texts do have something in common. They are both based on the assumption that God is sovereign. Even though God's reign is hard to see, it is the basic reality of the whole creation. In the 50s (C.E.), Nero was an able and just administrator; in the 90s, he became the head healed from a mortal blow (Rev. 13:3)–a fearsome specter back from the dead to make trouble for the church again. There is no more question of the Christian's doing good and being rewarded for it. The question becomes, "Who is like the beast, and who can fight against it?" (Rev. 13:4). The resounding and encouraging reply of the whole book of Revelation is that God is stronger than the beast and will fight against it and win.

A second underlying assumption of these texts is that the means of God's reign are dramatically different from the visible means of the beastly powers. Paul moved directly from the exhortation of respect for authority to the principle that one should "owe no one anything, except to love one another" (Rom. 13:8). Love, not violence, is the hallmark of the divine ruler. Revelation 13, with all its frightening bombast, leads to the saints singing the praises of the lamb accompanied by harp music. This is followed by angelic preachers proclaiming God's victory over fallen Babylon. God's subjects sing instead of quaking with fear; they preach instead of fighting. God rules with grace, and that does not change even in the face of fearsome violence. Just as the crucified Lord refused to use resurrection power to force the divine rule on people, so the people who follow that Lord do not fear the violence of the beast or respond with violence. These who follow the crucified Lord– refuse to force faith.

But politics is where the action is. Love, grace, worship, preaching, and holy living do not accomplish anything. Is that not what we hear from our age? Is that not what we often feel? It was not just a passing theme of the 1960s that said, the real action was in the streets, not in the pulpits. Something deep in the spirit of our age continues to nag us with that doubt. Worship of the slain lamb and preaching of God's grace seem to be so much whistling in the wind compared with politics. Still, in and behind our two texts stands the faith that God is at work in silent and unseen ways to bring about the transformation of "the kingdom of the world" into "the kingdom of our Lord and of his Messiah" (Rev. 11:15).

The challenge to the preacher and the teacher of preaching is to lead people to open the eyes of their faith to see the reality of God at work all around. We need to be like Elisha, who prayed that the eyes of his servant would be opened to see the forces of God assembled on the mountains. (2 Kings 6:15–17) This in no way means that we can somehow escape all influences of politics. We do live in the cities, counties, states, and nations of our world. We do have responsibilities to those necessary structures of authority. However, our primary responsibility is to the God of grace, whose servants we are and whose "power is made perfect in weakness" (2 Cor. 12:9). We live in what appears to be an oxymoronic state. In reality, we live in the tension between the fallen age of humanity and the redemptive purpose and power of God.

The question remains, How can preaching open the eyes of people living in this world to see the reality of God reigning? We pray, "Thy will be done on earth as it is in heaven." How do we help people see the heavenly side? These two texts show two different ways of doing this. Paul's approach is rather direct and didactic. He simply states that "there is no authority except from God, and those authorities that exist have been instituted by God." In a relatively safe, peaceful environment this approach seems to have worked. Its hidden danger is that Christians might be encouraged to obey rules and follow leaders that are directing people away from the will of God.

The apocalyptic approach portrays vividly the combat between the forces of God and those opposing God's reign. In a dangerous and violent environment, this approach seems to have worked. I taught a series of lessons on Revelation to a group of adults. One of them was a recent refugee from the persecution of Christians in Sudan. The apocalyptic imagery of our lessons spoke directly to him though to the rest of us it seemed to come from another world.

The gospels indicate that Jesus used didactic and apocalyptic approaches in different situations. In a deep sense, the whole Bible and the testimony of believers down through history offer us many texts and examples of how to communicate the reality of God. No single way will work for every situation; more than two exist. What is important is that preachers and other leaders talk openly about God. This seems like a truism, but many congregations experience a strange lack of theological language. Until people learn a vocabulary by which to think about and talk about the reality of the reign of God, we cannot expect them to actualize that reign in their lives. Until we give them words, stories, and images to connect with the reign and will of God in heaven, they will not be able to visualize the reign and will of God on earth. The fissure through which John the seer was able to trace the reality of God on the throne and God's faithful ones around the throne can be opened only by a courageous and imaginative use of language. The straight-on statements about the relationship of familiar authorities with God as the source of all authority might feel strange on our tongues, but they are vital to the life of faith, especially when confronted by powerful authorities.

In the last two paragraphs of Romans 13, Paul returns to a more general mode of exhortation. Verse 7 picks up on the theme of what we owe and leads to the principle of love, which Paul calls "the fulfilling of the law" (13:10). Any attempt to drive a wedge between Paul and Jesus runs aground on this passage. This is so similar to the wording of several teachings of Jesus found in the gospels that it appears that Paul must have been aware of those teachings. The surprise here is that Paul would quote the *Torah* at all, after what he writes in Romans 7:7–13. Paul was not out to destroy the law any more than Jesus was.

He was, rather, teaching that the law was not given as a way to become worthy of salvation but as a way to live once one has received the salvation available because of God's grace. Christ, he claims (Rom. 10:4), is "the end of the law." Here in chapter 13, Paul specifies love as the law's fulfillment, being careful to use two different words in the two references. The first of these verses points to Christ as the goal toward which the law was moving. The second spotlights love as the ethical principle, which fulfills any and all gaps in the commandments.

At this point, Paul pens the closing *inclusio* of this exposition—the final exhortation. He begins with another motivation for Christian living: eschatology. The warning that judgment day is coming is an important reminder for every Christian in any age. No matter how one thinks about the end time, every day brings us closer to our own end, whether that end is the cataclysmic coming of our Lord or the quiet death of the individual. It is absurd for we who believe in the Christ who will judge the living and the dead to be involved in any activity of which we would be ashamed at his appearing. The deeds and the things that belong to a temporary age should never command our primary loyalty. The deeds and the things that belong to the reign of evil should have no place at all in a Christian's life. In chapter 1, we observed Augustine's experience. When Augustine read these verses, his tears flowed in repentance for the years wasted in such living. From then on, his life became the living sacrifice Paul had described.

So we see that the dedicated and transformed Christian is expected to do more than enjoy his or her new life in the company of those who share the experience. That new life is to be lived in full view of and participation in the world in which we find ourselves—a world of people, some friendly and some mean; a world of temptations attractive and dangerous. But clothed with Christ, we can live in the world and overcome it. In the next chapter, we shall see how this applies to tension among believers.

For Further Reading

Furnish, Victor Paul. *The Moral Teaching of Paul.* Nashville: Abingdon Press, 1979.

———. *Theology and Ethics in Paul.* Nashville: Abingdon Press, 1968.

Hays, Richard B. *The Moral Vision of the New Testament: A Contemporary Introduction to New Testament Ethics.* San Francisco: Harper SanFrancisco, 1996.

CHAPTER 8

What Romans Says about Christian Relationships

As pointed out in the Introduction, Paul apparently had two separate, but related, objectives as he wrote this epistle to the Christians in Rome. He wrote both as a missionary hoping that these believers would become supporters of his mission to take the gospel to Spain and as a pastor concerned about the reported tensions among the believers in Rome. We will look at this latter concern in the present chapter.

Part of Paul's argument through the first eleven chapters has been to show that all people—Jews and Greeks—are on equal footing before God. Although the gospel came first to the Jews, it also came to the Greeks (Gentiles). All have sinned, and all can exercise the faith necessary to receive God's gracious forgiveness. Having established this soteriological base and having warned Jews and Gentiles of the danger of arrogance directed to one another (Rom. 9:30–33; 11:17–24), Paul turns in chapters 12–15 to more specific instruction on human relationships.

As we saw in the last chapter, Paul begins chapter 12 with a beautiful exhortation to self-sacrifice and transformation. He follows this with a description of the community of faith as one body with many members, emphasizing the various functions among the members. This sets up his direct advice in 12:9–21. A series of imperatives and participles follow one another in proverbial fashion. They give his advice in general about dealing positively and lovingly with people inside and outside the church.

Chapter 13 opens with advice concerning subjection to the governing authorities (*exousiais*). Christians should live in peace with their neighbors–including the structures of authority–so far as it depends on them (12:18). The chapter ends with a reminder that the law of love for neighbor summarizes all biblical commandments and leads us not to harm anybody. This exhortation receives added weight by being rooted in the eschatological expectation that should motivate the believer to demonstrate the hope in the coming salvation in the Lord Jesus Christ.

In chapter 14, Paul makes these instructions concrete. Paul is dealing with a serious division among the Christians in Rome. Chapter 16 makes it clear that even though he has never visited Rome, he has friends among the Roman believers. Thus, he has a number of potential sources of information about the problems of the church and knows some things about their Christian activities in Rome. The issues cited in the text indicate the sorts of disagreements causing tension. Scholars continue to try to deduce from chapters 14 and 15 the details of the problem and to identify the sides in these disagreements, but they have not reached a consensus.

We probably will never be sure whom Paul referred to as "the weak" or "the strong." To me, the division was likely related to the Jew-Gentile grouping in the aftermath of the expulsion of Jews from Rome by the emperor Claudius. This expulsion order was apparently precipitated when the Jewish population in Rome disturbed the peace with their activities opposing Christianity. Acts 18:2 indicates that Aquila and Priscilla met Paul in Corinth because they had been ordered out of Rome by this edict. These Jewish Christians were permitted to return only when Claudius died and Nero acceded to the imperial throne. During the years the Jewish Christians were missing from Rome, the new Gentile leaders likely changed aspects of church life in Rome. When the Jews were permitted to return, tension apparently arose over these changes.

This general scenario of tension is about as far as we can go in guessing about the groupings among the Roman Christians at the time Paul was writing. All we know for sure is that the general tension had come to a head around the issues of eating, drinking, and keeping special days. "Some believe in eating anything, while the weak eat only vegetables" (14:2). Verse 5 says, "Some judge one day to be better than another, while others judge all days to be alike." Whether it was kosher food versus unkosher food or Jewish holy days versus no holy days, we do not know. It could have been more complicated than that in a city where most meat was purchased at pagan temples (as in Corinth; see 1 Cor. 8–10) and where the religious and political calendars were full of special days. We should leave such details to history and look at Paul's advice that applies to any situations of division or tension among Christians.

Paul based his instruction about relationships among these people on two theoretical platforms: Christian theology and Christian anthropology. He erected these platforms on a number of brief statements.

"God has welcomed them" (14:3c). Since God has already accepted all of us into the heavenly family, we have no right to despise or pass judgment on one another. This is immediately followed by an anthropological description of fellow believers as "servants of another," not of humans, not even of believers, but of God. This first step concludes with, "the Lord is able to make them stand." God welcomes each, and God strengthens each; so, we should not judge our fellow servants of God.

In 14:5–6, we see that the believers act in honor of the Lord, even when their actions appear to conflict with one another. Verses 7–9 broaden this by pointing out that we do not live or die to ourselves but to the Lord, This section ends with a reminder that "to this end Christ died and lived again, so that he might be Lord of both the dead and the living." So the familiar statement, "It's my life" does not apply to the Christian. We live and we die to the Lord who lived and died and lives again for us.

Paul gets even more direct in 14:10–12, pointing out that "we will all stand before the judgment seat of God." So we should never attempt to pass judgment on our brothers or sisters.

We get the impression from 14:13 that Paul had finally begun preaching: "Let us therefore no longer pass judgment," but he seems almost to interrupt his exhortation with another theological statement, this time from his understanding of creation (14:14): "I know and am persuaded in the Lord Jesus that nothing is unclean [Greek: *koinon*] in itself." This is a radical statement from a former Pharisee. According to Acts 10–11 Peter received a vision showing him all kinds of beasts. He was told to kill and eat. Peter refused, saying, "By no means, Lord; for I have never eaten anything that is profane [*koinon*] or unclean [*akatharton*]." He heard the reply, "What God has made clean, you must not call profane." This happened three times before Peter was ready to receive the invitation to preach the gospel to a Gentile. Paul's upbringing was stricter than Peter's, so for him to say nothing was unclean in itself was a huge step away from his strict Jewish food laws. Some of the Jewish Christians in Rome had not likely come that far in their new covenant faith, but Paul stated it as his personal position "in the Lord Jesus."

He returns to the exhortation in a way reminiscent of 13:10: love does no harm to the neighbor. Here the argument seems to do an about face. Paul appears to imply that this fuss about kosher food is nonsense. In verse 15, he turns on those who were eating everything: "Do not let what you eat cause the ruin of one for whom Christ died." Paul applies Christian theological anthropology to ethics. Since he has already established the belief that Christ died for sinners, we are left no way out except to recognize that these people with whom we disagree are recipients of the grace of God in Christ just as we are.

In 14:17–18, Paul rolls out the big guns. He relates the whole situation to the reign of God, the Holy Spirit, service to Christ, acceptability to God, and approval by other humans. His ethical conclusion (v. 19) is simple yet profound: "Let us then pursue what makes for peace and for mutual upbuilding." He follows this with another reminder of creation theology: "Do not for the sake of food, destroy the work of God" (14:20). He reemphasizes his conviction that everything is clean (kosher, Greek: *kathara*). Still, he insists that it is wrong to harm another, and especially to endanger another's relationship with God, by what one eats. Verse 21 states this in another way: it is better to abstain from what you are free to eat than to cause a brother or sister to stumble. Verses 22 and 23 tie all this in with the individual's faith. That faith is something between the individual and God. So we should honor each one's personal faith and each one's personal doubts and not cause anybody to act contrary to his or her faith.

The closing sentence in this passage is a ringing redefinition: "whatever does not proceed from faith is sin." Up to this point, Paul has treated sin as disobedience of a command, thinking in terms of Adam's sin, especially as it contrasted with Christ's radical obedience. Now, however, he deals with the relationship of one believer to another and has to nuance his understanding of sin. In the realm of human relationships, one can damage another without doing something forbidden. We know from experience that acts done with the best of intentions can be misunderstood or imitated by the wrong person. That is what Paul deals with here. He points out to one and all that actions done in spite of one's conscience or faith create the guilt of sin in the person who acts outside his or her personal faith.

So what are we/they to do? Chapter 15 opens with the demand, "We who are strong ought to put up with the failings of the weak." This is immediately rooted in the community ("please our neighbor") and in Christ ("did not please himself"). Once again Paul bases his relational exhortation on theology, in this case, the example of Christ himself. His principle of imitating Christ (see 1 Cor. 11:1, which ends the same sort of exhortation as in Rom. 14–15) works well at this point. Paul has already pointed out (5:6–11) that Christ died for us "while we were still weak." He uses the same word in 5:6 (*asthenon*) to describe all of us in our need of justification as he used in 15:1 to describe the failings or weaknesses (*asthenemata*) of the weak (*adunatoi*). Paul once again puts all believers on the same level. The only reason we can claim any strength is that Christ sacrificed his strength to die for us in our weakness. For us to tolerate the weaknesses of our Christian sisters and brothers should not be seen as a great sacrifice.

This ends Paul's argument but not his sermon. In 15:5–6, he offers a prayer for God's help in Christians' living in harmony with one another so that they "may with one voice glorify the God and Father of our Lord Jesus Christ." Paul reminds his readers that all we do is based on God's character. The God Paul points to here is the God of steadfastness and encouragement. If God is our solid foundation and our cheerleader, we ought to be able to tolerate differences of opinion among those who trust in this God. Paul also connects this exposition in relation to Christ Jesus, who (he already said) did not live to please himself.

A closing exhortation refers back to the section's beginning. Paul challenges the readers to "Welcome one another, therefore, just as Christ has welcomed you." This would take their attention back to 14:3: "God has welcomed them." Paul's final word on this subject refers to how Christ has worked the will of God in bringing the Gentiles to the glorification of God. He quotes Psalm 18:49; Deuteronomy 32:43; Psalm 117:1; and Isaiah 11:10 from the Septuagint (LXX), which differs in places from the Hebrew text used by the NRSV translators. He prays for their joy, peace, and hope. This is one of several places where Paul quotes passages from all three divisions of the Hebrew Bible: *Torah,* Writings, and Prophets. If Christ can fulfill the scriptures that declare the unity of Jews and Gentiles under God's sovereignty, surely these Roman believers could unite in spite of their differences of opinion.

All this scripture is followed by another prayer—a sort of benediction that parallels verses 5 and 6 in an interesting way. The earlier one pointed to steadfastness and encouragement as characteristics of God, and this one points to hope. The earlier one connected them with Christ Jesus, and this one with the Holy Spirit. Between the two are texts from the three divisions of the Hebrew Bible. Paul could not have put more authoritative emphasis on his exhortation in these chapters than he did with a conclusion that sandwiches the whole of scripture between two prayers that refer to God, Christ, and the Holy Spirit.

Can we learn something from Paul's way of dealing with tension among Christians? In every case, we should go back to the basics. In the heat of disagreements, we need to be reminded of our theological foundations:

- The love and sovereignty of God
- Our standing before God
- The price Christ has paid for each of us
- The empowering presence of the Holy Spirit
- The nature of individual faith
- Our purpose and ultimate goal as Christians

Then we can turn to our disagreements to see if they are worth fighting about. Most of them are not. When we decide that an open disagreement is necessary, we should treat one another as works of God, those for whom Christ died, and those in whom the Holy Spirit is working.

We should affirm here that Paul was not generally "wishy-washy" in doctrine or morals. Paul could state matters absolutely when he saw that something essential was at stake. The ancient slogan, "In essentials unity, in non-essentials liberty, and in all things charity (or love)" describes quite well Paul's dealing with such matters. The difficulty lies in deciding which is which. Paul was convinced that rules about food or special days had nothing to do with our salvation except when used to cause others to fall from faith. Therefore, Christians should be willing to tolerate differences of opinion and practice for such actions. We must be willing to sacrifice our freedom to act legitimately when we see that our actions are hurting another believer. Do these principles solve all our problems? Obviously not. However, they can go a long way toward guiding us to live in harmony within the family of God.

For Further Reading

Banks, Robert. *Paul's Idea of Community.* Grand Rapids: W. B. Eerdmans, 1980.

Murphy-O'Connor, Jerome. *Becoming Human Together.* Wilmington, Del.: Michael Glazier, 1984.

Theissen, Gerd. *The Social Setting of Pauline Christianity.* Philadelphia: Fortress Press, 1982.

PART 2

Sermons on Challenging Texts in Romans

CHAPTER 9

Preaching from Romans
1:18—3:26

Romans 1:1–17 contains the address, identification of the author, and introduction of the theme typical of a first century Greek letter. Verses 16–17 indicate that Paul was beginning to write about the gospel, which (see vv. 1–4) he had been called to serve. Thus we can expect the composition of at least the first part of the letter will be gospel logic—that is, the author will present his thoughts in an order appropriate to the presentation of the good news of the grace of God in Christ Jesus.

Therefore, we should not be surprised that 1:18 begins a treatment of sin. After all, if the personal result of the reception of the gospel is the forgiveness of sin, the most appropriate way to prepare people to receive the gospel is to convince them of their need of it. This is what we find in Romans 1:18–3:20.

If Paul seems to spend too much energy on sin, perhaps we should check our own attitudes toward evil in the world. Have we become so callused by our culture that we no longer take sin seriously? Are we concerned that our preaching might be seen as too negative if we dwell on sin? Even the lectionary reflects this unwillingness to deal with sin. The epistle reading for the ninth Sunday of Epiphany in Year A is Romans 1:16–17 and 3:22–31. This covers the good news while skipping the bad. None of the commonly-used lectionaries include a reading from 1:18–3:21.

As we shall see, Paul took sin seriously because he recognized that God took sin seriously. Romans 1:18 presents the wrath of God as the first aspect of God's righteousness being revealed in the gospel. Just as we shy away from dealing with sin, we tend to favor other characteristics of God over wrath. This aversion to the negative is a typical American attitude. The result is too often negative instead of positive: When we do not hold the mirror of righteousness before our people to draw their attention to their sin, we cause them to miss seeing the depth of God's love and grace in Jesus Christ. If our depiction of God is that of an indulgent uncle, our people might enjoy but will hardly respect God.

Look at the extensive view of sin in these chapters. Paul returns to the subject in chapters 5, 6, and 7, but he deals with the reality and universality of sin at the beginning of his letter. In chapter 1, Paul pictures sin as it existed among the Gentiles. He removes any appeal to ignorance by pointing out (vv. 19–21) that everybody has had the revelation of God in the creation. He claims that everybody has known God's "eternal power and divine nature." ever since the creation (v. 20). We have no excuse, then, for the decision to neglect the worship of God and to turn instead to the glorification and representations of creatures.

The result of this rebellion is that "God gave them up." This statement appears three times here (vv. 24, 26, and 28), with identical wording each time. Each time what appears to be a list of sinful activities follows. However, these lists, or catalogs, of sins are stated as results of sin. The basic sin (original sin?) is the refusal to glorify the Creator and the rebellious worship of creatures instead. Everything else on the sin list represents detailed and destructive results of sin. God gave the human race over to these results.

Chapter 2 highlights those who might think they are better than the people described in chapter 1. Paul aims explicitly at his fellow Jews, but at first he employs more general wording: "whoever you are, when you judge others." He points out that such human judges are hypocritical since they (we?) do the same things they accuse others of doing. In 2:7–10, Paul indicates that people will be judged according to their actions.

He makes it clear that because all commit sin, all are liable to a judgment of "guilty." At this point, he repeats the phrase he first used in 1:16: "the Jew first and also the Greek." In 1:16 the power of God for salvation is available to both. Here both Jew and Greek face both negative (v. 9) and positive (v. 10) possibilities. Paul is driving toward his first big conclusion by showing that Jews and Greeks are in danger of God's condemnation.

In 2:12–16, Paul looks at the equality of Jew and Gentile from another angle: Gentiles have consciences that are equivalent to a law (or *Torah*) written on their hearts, as will be shown in the eschatological judgment. Verse 17 turns explicitly to the Jews, showing that they have no reason to think they are superior to the Gentiles with regard to sin and righteousness. Verses 17–20 list the categories by which the Jews contrasted themselves with the Gentiles, and verses 21–24 demonstrate that the Jews transgress every one of these categories.

Even circumcision is valueless for those who do not live out the law (vv. 25–29). Paul takes on the spirit of the prophets as he argues that the value of circumcision is spiritual and that the physical reality guarantees nothing if it is not backed up by the life. This leads to the question with which Paul opens chapter 3: "Then what advantage has the Jew?" Paul could think of many advantages, the first being that they have been "entrusted with the oracles of God." Paul does not mention other advantages until he dictates chapter 9. His primary concern here is sin's pervasiveness, so he discusses the relationship of human sin to God's righteousness. Then he lists a chain of scripture quotations (vv. 10–18) followed by echoes of several other scripture texts, ending with verse 20: "through the law comes the knowledge of sin." This sets up Paul's turn to the good news.

Romans 3:21–26 is the first summary passage in the epistle. In each of these passages, Paul reminds his hearers/readers of what he has just dealt with and then indicates where he intends to go next. Verses 21–22*a* proclaim the good news against the background of the reality and universality of sin in the world: "But now, apart from the law, the righteousness of God has been disclosed, and is attested by the law and the prophets, the righteousness of God through faith in Jesus Christ for all who believe."

Paul has shown the inability of the law (*Torah*) to make the Jews righteous, as he had shown that people without the *Torah* cannot live righteous lives by their own criteria. So another way is needed. This new way (God's righteousness/justification) has been shown to the world, having been witnessed to by both the law (*Torah*) and prophets (see 1:2). This way is personal, by means of the faithfulness of Jesus Christ. Here I find fault with most translations of Romans, and an increasing number of scholars are joining the critique.[1] The Greek word *pistis* can mean faith or faithfulness/loyalty. In verse 22, Paul links *pistis* with the genitive form of Jesus Christ. This construction can be translated "through faith in Jesus Christ" or "by means of the faithfulness of Jesus Christ." The latter (reading the genitive as subjective/possessive) seems to me to be the most natural reading. This reading is further supported by the next part of the sentence: "for all who believe." This phrase obviously refers to the human believers. That would make the former phrase redundant if we take it as an objective genitive ("through faith in Jesus Christ"). I understand Paul to be saying that God's new process (apart from the *Torah*) is through the instrumentality of the faithful/obedient life and death of Jesus (see 6:12–21). Justification is made accessible for us human beings by our faith/faithfulness (in relation to Jesus).

Paul forges ahead in verse 23 with the insistence that this justification is available to *all* who believe. He ties this to the reminder of his completed argument: For the need of forgiveness, no distinction separates humans "since all have sinned and fall short of the glory of God." This mention again of "glory" should remind us of Paul's connection of "glory" with the result of sin and the hope of restoration, as we have seen in Chapter 5. The verb here usually translated as "fall short of" (*hysterountai*) can be better translated as "lack." Paul never clearly uses "glory" as a target that our lives fall short of. He never indicates that our lives should be like God's life. He understood "glory" as a characteristic we received when God created us. We lost this "glory" as a result of sin, but God will restore it to us in the eschaton. (See chapter 3.)

Paul emphasizes that these sinners are justified by the gift of God's grace by means of the redemption that is in Christ Jesus (the construction parallels that in v. 22). The faithfulness of Jesus parallels the redemption in Jesus, "whom God put forward as a sacrifice of atonement by his blood, effective through faith." The word translated as "sacrifice of atonement" is the word *hilasterion.* The LXX used *hilasterion* to translate the Hebrew *kapporet,* the covering or "mercy seat" of the ark of the covenant in the holy of holies of the Jerusalem temple. This was the place where on the Day of Atonement the high priest sprinkled the blood of a bull and a goat for his own sins and the sins of the people. As Leviticus 16 makes clear, this is the nearest a human being can get to the presence of God. For that reason only, the high priest could approach it, and he could do so only one day a year.

So Paul's description here of God putting Jesus forward as *hilasterion* indicates not only Jesus' connection with the sacrifice of atonement, but also his representing the presence of God among God's people as One who forgives and redeems. This is done "by his blood." Thus, Christ is the blood of the sacrifice and the presence of God to receive the sacrifice. Such a double metaphor might seem odd to us, but it appears not to have seemed strange to the early Christians. Hebrews 9 and 10 uses a similar multiple metaphor when it presents Christ as the high priest (Hebrews 10:21), as the source of the blood sacrifice (9:12), and as the veil of the temple through which the high priest carried the blood into the presence of God (10:20).

What is the point to all this? Romans 3:25*b*-26 indicates that this makes our justification possible. It defends God's righteousness since indulgent forgiveness would indicate God's weakness instead of God's justice. On this side of the blood of Jesus, we can see God as both the justifier and the just one, since this God who demanded sacrifice has provided the sacrifice (compare this with Gen. 22, the "binding of Isaac").

In the sermon that follows, I have tried to deal with sin as something we are familiar with but which we try to overlook or explain away. I attempt to show how seriously God takes sin and what God in Christ has done to lift the burden of sin from us.

SERMON ▰▰▰▰▰▰▰▰▰▰▰▰▰▰▰▰▰▰▰▰▰▰▰▰▰▰▰▰▰▰▰▰▰▰▰

"What Have I Done?
(Romans 3:9–26)

Introduction

The disciples asked at the table of the Last Supper: "Surely not I!" (Mk. 14:19). We sing, "Was it for crimes that I have done He groaned upon the tree?" ("At the Cross") The answer to both is "YES!" He "was handed over to death for our trespasses" (Rom. 4:25).

1. Sin Is the Cause of the Human Predicament

1. Among the first questions that come to mind when bad things happen to us is, "Why did this happen to me?" We easily forget the primary cause of evil, pain, and sorrow in our lives.

2. Karl Menninger put the question in the title of a book: *Whatever Became of Sin?*[2]

3. We justify sin by blaming a complicated situation.

4. We rename sin as antisocial behavior.

5. We shift the blame for sin to parents. In Leonard Bernstein's "West Side Story," some street toughs sing, "I'm depraved because I'm deprived."[3]

6. One woman I ministered to kept asking why her son had died, when the immediate cause was an overdose of illicit drugs he had obtained by stealing them.

7. Down deep we are all like Lady Macbeth, trying to wash off the stain of our sin.

8. Psychiatrists think they see the depths of evil in the analysis of the human psyche, but we see it most darkly at the cross of Jesus.

2. Sin Is the Cause of Christ's Crucifixion

The theme of human sin runs through the records of passion week:

1. It begins at the triumphal entry with voices praising Jesus and ends with voices calling "crucify him!"
2. The cleansing of the temple shows religious sin.
3. The conspiracy to kill Jesus shows political sin.
4. Judas's betrayal of Jesus shows individual disloyalty.
5. Peter, James, and John falling asleep in the garden shows a weakness of the flesh.
6. The disciples' forsaking Jesus and fleeing shows a failure of nerve.
7. Peter's denial shows human panic in stress.
8. Pilate washing his hands shows us that not to decide is to decide.
9. The soldiers beating, mocking, and nailing Jesus to the cross shows human insensitivity.
10. In the narrative of passion week, we see violence, illegality, perjury, irresponsibility, weakness—it's all there!
11. *They* crucified "The King of the Jews," but the question keeps returning: "Lord, is it I?"
12. God's answer appears like a superscription emblazoned across the sky over Golgotha in 2000 languages: "All have sinned and lack the glory of God."

3. And Yet Christ Is the Cause of Our Escape from Sin

"While we still were sinners Christ died for us" (Rom. 5:8).

Because we were sinners Christ died for us.

To forgive us sinners Christ died for us.

READ: Isaiah 53:4–6.

Conclusion

The greatest "Who done it?" of all time is no mystery at all. *We did it.* We caused Christ's cruel death. Yet God did it and made it the greatest, most profound mystery of all. Christ did not just die. He stormed the gates of Hades and died our death for us. He conquered death with the power of life itself. So we do not mourn here today, but in awe and repentance, *we celebrate life!*

CHAPTER 10

Preaching from Romans 4:1–25[1]

In Romans 4, Paul deals with the meaning and nature of faith. This was the appropriate place for him to do this, since he has established (in 3:22) that justification is offered to sinners through the faith(fullness) of Jesus to all who have faith. This word *pistis* (faith, faithful, loyalty) is a Greek term with multiple meanings, especially for those who were aware of its use in the LXX translation of the Hebrew Scriptures. Instead of offering a philosophical or etymological definition of faith/faithfulness, Paul refers to a story familiar to all who knew the scripture—the story of Abraham and Sarah. Abraham was the ultimate patriarch of the Hebrews—the model of the obedience of faith. Because he was the first recipient of circumcision as the sign of the covenant (Gen. 17:24), he was the exemplary, faithful Jew.

The form of Paul's argument here is *midrash*–the Jewish hermeneutical/homiletical form. Midrash typically takes a *Torah* text, couples it with a text from another part of scripture (called *Haftarah*), and explains its application to life in the present. In this case the *Torah* text is Genesis 15:6; the other text is Psalm 32:1–2*a*. The two texts are combined on the basis of one Hebrew word they have in common: the verb (*chashav*) translated "to reckon." Paul could have preached this chapter as a sermon in a synagogue.

97

The question in Paul's mind here is: Was Abraham justified by works of the law or by faith? If by faith, then Abraham is the model of faith not only for the Jew but also for the Greek. That is precisely Paul's conclusion. The first step in Paul's argument is a look at the meaning of this reckoning as righteous. The Genesis 15 text states that Abraham's faith was reckoned to him as righteousness. Since the Greek word for "righteousness" is the same as that translated "justification," for Paul, to be reckoned righteous was equivalent to being justified. He further indicates that since it was reckoned so freely, it was not a wage but a gift.

Next, Paul examines what justification amounts to. Psalm 32 uses the term "reckon" in reference to forgiveness of sins. That indicates that the biblical writers have long understood justification as applying to sinners and not to those already righteous. Paul then asks whether this justification happened before or after Abraham's circumcision (the work of the law par excellence). The answer is, of course, before. Abraham's circumcision is recorded in Genesis 17, where the promise of God is renewed and Abraham's name is changed from Abram. At this point Paul has established, by a simple historical question, that the ground of Abraham's justification by God was his faith and not his legal works. This makes Abraham the ancestor of all who have the same kind of faith.

The last part of the chapter deals with the nature of that faith. Paul connects faith with the promise of God. Promise appears to have been a primary category by which the early church understood the nature of the gospel. In Luke's report of Peter's Pentecost sermon in the temple, Peter concludes, "For the promise is for you, for your children, and for all who are far away, everyone whom the Lord our God calls to him" (Acts 2:39). Ephesians 3:6 states, "the Gentiles have become fellow heirs, members of the same body, and sharers in the promise in Christ Jesus through the gospel."

The aspect of God's promise to Abraham that Paul emphasizes is that of universal promise ("that he would inherit the world"; 4:13). That this promise rests on faith in the giver of the promise makes Abraham's experience applicable to all people. Following several statements about Abraham's belief,

Paul digs to the heart of the matter in verse 21: "being fully convinced that God was able to do what he had promised." In other words, faith is taking God at God's word.

Embedded in this *midrash* are three statements about this God whose promise is trustworthy. Verse 5 points to the object of Abraham's trust as "him who justifies the ungodly." Verse 17 describes God as the one "who gives life to the dead and calls into existence the things that do not exist." Verse 24 points to the God "who raised Jesus our Lord from the dead." The justifier is a judge, and the giver of life is a creator. Finally, the one who raised Jesus from the dead ("for our sins...for our justification") is the gracious Creator-Judge. His word brings forth not only the physical creation but also the righteousness so lacking among human beings.

It is not just faith in general that accomplishes justification. It is only the faith(fulness) of the Creator-Judge God and Jesus Christ our Lord that makes it possible. Our faith(fulness) is the means by which we can access this gracious forgiveness that makes us (re-creates us) righteous. Paul's use of the Abraham story here indicates the importance of what we call the Old Testament for our Christian formation. Paul's insistence that "...the words, 'it was reckoned to him,' were written not for his sake alone, but for ours also," are not a license for wild allegory or direct anachronistic application. Paul's practice teaches us that the Hebrew Scriptures were the Bible of the early church and should be studied carefully by Christians today.

Most scholars read verse 25 as probably an early Christian confession of faith or even part of an early hymn. The Greek is nicely phrased and balanced:

hos paredothe dia ta paraptomata hemon

kai egerthe dia ten dikaiosin hemon

who was handed over for our trespasses

and raised up for our justification.

Romans 1:3–4 is another such passage. In reading these statements about Christ and the gospel, we are touching the heart of the faith of the earliest Christians. We should join their song with great reverence.

In the following sermon I describe faith that is radical and base the description on the object of faith—the God who is able and willing to do outlandish things for believers.

SERMON ▰▰▰▰▰▰▰▰▰▰▰▰▰▰▰▰▰▰▰▰▰▰▰▰▰▰▰▰▰

The Power Of Faith
(Romans 4)

Introduction

Faith is not determination, not self-confidence, not individual ability. No matter how able we are, "our best" will prove not good enough. Faith is recognizing our inability and accepting the help available from God.

1. Faith Makes Real for Us the Powerful Promise of God (4:16, 21)

1. Abraham expected the impossible, and God delivered.
2. Christ promised unbelievable things.
3. Read the Beatitudes, Matthew 4:3–11.
4. Read John 14:12–14, "I will do whatever you ask..."
5. In faith, we take God at God's word. In faith, we expect that God will deliver. In faith, we fulfill our conditions for that delivery. In faith, we expect that even God's most outlandish promise will be delivered: John 14:16–17– The Holy Spirit.

2. Faith Makes Real for Us the Powerful Presence of God (4:17b)

1. God's promises are powerful because in promising, God commits God's-self.
2. If God is really in you, the only limits to what you can do are God's will and your will.
3. Do you believe this? If so, then put it into practice.

Conclusion

One of the most damaging traditions alive in the church teaches us that as soon as the New Testament was written, God's direct power was withdrawn. This leads many Christians not to expect God to work in a powerful way today. Either God is at work today, or Christianity is a farce! If God is not working in our lives and in our church, then we are to be pitied. But God's word says that God is at work. The experience of the church says that God is at work. You can live not only in a promise, but also in a power. Let God work in you. Be "fully convinced that God [is] able to do what he...promised." Let the power of God in the presence of God work through your faith today.

CHAPTER 11

Preaching from Romans 5:1–11[1]

In these verses from Romans 5, we find one of Paul's typical summary statements. Paul reminds his audience what he has shown so far ("Therefore, since we are justified by faith"), and then proceeds to show what this means in terms of their present status. In doing so, Paul completes the glossary of salvation terminology he began in chapter 3. Justification is Paul's umbrella term for what we usually refer to as salvation. As we saw in chapter 4, this was a legal (courtroom) term for Paul. In 3:24–25, he listed redemption and atonement. Here in chapter 5, he adds peace, access, hope, love, salvation, and reconciliation.

These terms provide plenty of grist for the sermon mill though the preacher should be careful not to sound too theological with them. In fact, Paul was pulling terms from a variety of semantic domains to constitute this list. Redemption came from the business world, especially in the context of slavery, where a slave was often bought from a master and at times bought himself from that master to be set free.

The term translated as "sacrifice of atonement" is the single Greek word *hilasterion*. The LXX translators used this noun for the Hebrew word *kapporet*. The Hebrew term referred to the covering of the ark of the covenant in the holy of holies of the Jerusalem temple. Here on each Day of Atonement, the high priest brought the blood of the sacrifice of atonement and sprinkled it on the *hilasterion,* thus approaching as near to the presence of God as humanly possible. In other words, God presents Christ as the representative of God's presence among the people to receive the blood of atonement. Since Paul followed this term with "by his blood," it is clear that he thought of Jesus as the atoning sacrifice and the welcoming presence of God receiving the sacrifice. This is the one religious term Paul used in his glossary of salvation.

In 5:1 Paul promises that since all he said about salvation is true, we have peace with God. Paul's concept of peace, a relational term, certainly included more than the absence of hostility. The Hebrew word for peace is the familiar *shalom.* It carries the connotation of spiritual and physical wholeness that permeates all of life. The Romans would likely think of the *pax Romana,* which kept them from fear of invading armies and pirates but did not help with their fear of the stars, demons, fates, and other spiritual entities.

Along with peace comes access to grace. *Charis* meant much more to Paul than just God's saving mercy. Grace means the privilege of the presence of God in all aspects of life. Grace means the privilege of serving God by extending the reign of God (Eph. 3:7). Access to God's grace is the greatest of all privileges—the permission to approach the throne of God without prior invitation. In the court of an oriental despot such approach was a capital crime (see Esth. 4:11). In contrast to that, Paul indicated that we "stand" in that grace. God's grace is where the Christian lives and finds his or her stability.

So we have something to boast about—"our hope of sharing the glory of God." In chapter 5, we saw how important the word *glory* was for Paul. The human race has lost that glory as a result of sin, but here we have hope that it will be restored to us. But we also boast (Paul could not stay positive too long while using a term like boast) of suffering. Here he begins a chain of steps in the growth of character. "Suffering produces endurance." This is true for the Christian who continues in hope, but a preacher should not make this a general promise. Suffering produces bitterness, depression, broken relationships, and suicide in some people. However, the person who stands in grace and enjoys the peace of God sees suffering as another of those great privileges of serving the Lord.

Endurance produces character. When God is at work in a life, such work becomes obvious to those who observe the life. Character produces hope, which brings us full circle. Hope at this end of the chain is not wishful thinking. This kind of hope "does not disappoint us, because God's love has been poured into our hearts." We stand in God's grace; God's love is poured into our hearts; the Holy Spirit has been given to us. It is nearly too much to comprehend. We can only repeat it, believe it, and live it.

Verses 6–11 cover the same ground, this time spelling out in greater detail the implications of the faithfulness of Jesus Christ. The first three of these verses give us one of the most poignant pictures we have of Jesus' faithfulness on our behalf. We were weak, we were ungodly, and we were sinners. In spite of that, or because of that, "Christ died for us." This proves God's love for us.

Verse 9 parallels verse 1. In verse 1, Paul said, "since we are justified by faith we have peace with God." Verse 9 echoes, "Much more surely then, now that we have been justified by his blood, will we be saved through him from the wrath of God." Does this mean "by faith" is the same as "by his blood?" I suggest this is the case since *pistis* probably refers here to the faithfulness of Christ. His faith is spelled out in verses 6–8 and abbreviated in verse 9 with the words "by his blood." The result in verse 9 is our future salvation from God's wrath, whereas in verse 1 it is "peace with God." Little distinction exists between these two thoughts. To have peace with God is the positive way to express the more negative to be saved from God's wrath.

Paul then shows the extreme change this process of justification brings. We were enemies, but now we have been reconciled to God. That means we will be saved by his life. That gives us something to boast about. The Christian's boasting has nothing to do with our own abilities or accomplishments. We "boast in God through our Lord Jesus Christ, through whom we have received reconciliation."

So we see how extensive the glossary of salvation is. This glossary appears here in one of Paul's most intensive passages. The passage functions as a summary of God's justification by means of the death and resurrection of Christ. It hints at what is to come as the result of this justification. Thus, we have the central focus of the gospel, a fulcrum of Paul's gospel logic.

The following sermon was preached on the Sunday following Christmas, but its ideas fit any time of the year to remind people of the importance of what God has done and is doing for and in them.

SERMON ▬▬▬▬▬▬▬▬▬▬▬▬▬▬▬▬▬▬▬▬▬▬▬▬▬

The Greatest Gift
(Romans 5:1–11)

Introduction

Well, here we are just a few days after Christmas. I imagine many of you have Christmas gifts with you this morning–some article of clothing or jewelry, perhaps a watch or even a toy of some sort. We prize those gifts, far beyond their monetary value, because we connect them with the giver and our relationship with that person. Christmas is a season for gifts. This is appropriate because at this time we are reminded of God's greatest gift–Jesus Christ. The value of that gift also goes far beyond that of a miraculous birth of a baby in Bethlehem so long ago. Its value grows because of his life and even more because of his death and resurrection.

I want to think with you this morning about that gift, as the apostle Paul describes its value in Romans 5:1–11. To appreciate what he says there we should first read the verse that precedes those; 4:25 says that he "was handed over to death for our trespasses and was raised for our justification." The way the Christ child becomes a gift for us is that God has chosen to see the death of Jesus as an offering for our sins and the resurrection of Jesus as the seal of our salvation.

Read 5:1–11

1. By this gift God has justified us.

   - On the basis of our faith in and obedience of the risen Lord, God says, "You are innocent."
   - This is no semantic game, no funny celestial book-keeping, no deluding or pretending.
   - This is a word of redemption from the Creator. The One who said, "Let there be light," creates by declaring.
   - Therefore, you *are* innocent. God says so. It *is* so. Thus, we can sing full voiced the old gospel song, "What a wonderful change in my life has been wrought, since Jesus came into my heart."[2]

2. By this gift God has made peace with us.

   - Once we were sinners; now we are righteous people, saints even.
   - Once we were servants of Satan; now we are subjects of the Kingdom of Heaven.
   - Once we were enemies of God; now we are God's friends.
   - Once we were outcasts; now we are God's children.
   - Therefore, you are reconciled to God.

3. By this gift God has given us hope.

We have the hope of God's glory.

   - That glory was built into us humans in original creation.
   - That glory was lost when our human ancestors rebelled against God and disobeyed God's command.
   - That glory is lost for each of us when we follow their example and sin against God.
   - God has restored that glory through the redemption he makes possible through Jesus Christ.
   - God promises the full restoration of that glory for us who believe when the world is called to its end.

- Hope of glory means that we can cope with today, knowing there is a tomorrow. "Because he lives, I can face tomorrow."[3]
- Hope of glory means we can grow even when life deals us troubles, knowing God has an even greater gift waiting for us.
- Hope of glory means we can rejoice even in sufferings, knowing that these sufferings are not to be compared to the coming glory.
- Therefore, you have the hope of the glory of God.

4. By this gift, God has poured love into our hearts.

- We have talked about faith in what God has already done and hope for what God will do. We come to the present experience: not just "pie in the sky by and by" but love in the heart here and now.
- Love is the present, practical result of God's great gift. Even the secular world knows that what it needs is "love, sweet love."[4]
- The primary characteristic of the early church is summed up in the sentence: "Behold how they love one another."
- Love continues to be the make-or-break point for church growth no matter how it is defined and measured. The loving fellowship of the redeemed attracts people, wins people, keeps people, and transforms people.
- The community of love is the major occupation of the Holy Spirit. This is shown throughout the book of Acts and is testified to by Christians down through the history of the church.

Therefore, you are loved and can love others, too.

Conclusion

God could have sought revenge through the resurrection of Jesus. God could have brought the world to its knees immediately. But praise be, God chose rather to justify, to reconcile, to offer hope and love; for as we, in faith, receive those aspects of God's greatest gift, we enter the stream of the power of the Creator of the universe. Nothing can overcome us as long as we allow nothing to separate us from the love of God in Christ Jesus our Lord.

CHAPTER 12

Preaching from Romans 8:1–17[1]

Romans 8 brings us back into the sunshine after the clouds of chapter 7. Paul paints in vivid but dark colors the tension in the life of the Christian who wants to please God under her or his own power. Chapter 8 does the job by introducing the Holy Spirit's availability and power. Paul signals the change with this sentence, "There is therefore now no condemnation for those who are in Christ Jesus." He points to the continuing sunshine by closing the chapter with the promise that nothing "will be able to separate us from the love of God in Christ Jesus our Lord."

Such assurance is based in the past and in the present in verses 1–17 and in the present and future in 18–39. The first eight verses portray the redemption God has accomplished in Christ and its effects on the Christian life. The ringing declaration of hope ("no condemnation") is based on the liberation God accomplished in Christ. Once again, Paul contrasts life in Christ with life before Christ. He characterizes life before Christ as dominated by "the law of sin and of death." We can understand law here as principle since he refused in chapter 7 to identify the *Torah* with sin. This verse makes no contrast between law and no law. The contrast is, rather, between "the law of sin and death" and "the law of the Spirit of life in Christ Jesus."

Next Paul points to the life and death of Jesus as the means God used to overcome sin once for all. Even the law (meaning the *Torah*) could not accomplish this since it was dependent on human obedience, conditioned by fleshly weakness. But God sent the divine "Son in the likeness of sinful flesh, and to deal with sin." In chapter 7, Paul taught that the flesh is that aspect of the person where sin is able to gain a foothold to begin its military-like march to conquer the whole person. Sin as a power could be overcome only if God could destroy it in its stronghold, the human flesh. So it is "in the likeness of sinful flesh" that Christ was sent "to deal with sin", that is, as a sacrifice for sin. Thus, in Jesus' sacrificial act, God "condemned sin in the flesh." If God could not deal with sin at its strongest place, we were without hope. God attacked sin exactly there and "condemned" it. Those in Christ Jesus face no condemnation because through Christ Jesus, God has condemned sin and thus set us free from sin's rule.

The result of this redemption is that we "who...walk according to the Spirit" have "the just requirement of the law" fulfilled in us. God in Christ met the requirement of a blood sacrifice for sins. Now that sacrifice is bearing fruit in lives free from the bondage to sin. Verses 5 through 8 go into some detail about what it means to change life's point of orientation from the flesh to the Spirit. As he showed in the previous chapter, Paul was aware of the ever-present danger of our trying to live without the Spirit's power. With these verses, he warns people to keep their minds set (*phronema*) on the Spirit since the only alternative is the flesh, which "is hostile to God" and "cannot please God."

Now we turn to the work of the Spirit. Paul does this in verses 9–11, while at the same time destroying any possibility of our systematizing the Spirit as we would so often like to do. A quick look at the various ways he refers to the Spirit in these verses should cure us of ever trying to get the Spirit packaged neatly for human use:

1. The Spirit
2. The Spirit of God
3. The Spirit of Christ
4. Christ in you

5. The Spirit

6. The Spirit of him who raised Jesus from the dead

7. He who raised Christ from the dead

8. His Spirit

In three verses, he refers to the Spirit eight times, using seven different terms. There is no systematic Trinitarian formula, only references to divine power. This is the power of creation, the power of resurrection, the power of redemption, the power we need to keep us on the right track, and as he will show in the next paragraph, the power of adoption.

We have seen what God did in Christ to free us from the guilt of our sin. We have seen what God does in the Spirit to help us live free from sin. Now, in verses 12–17 Paul defines what this means about our status with God. Free from any debt to sin and on the road of life, how do we relate to God? "All who are led by the Spirit of God are children of God." It is appropriate in our age to translate the Greek word "sons" (*huioi*) as children to show that it applies to males and females. However, in Paul's day using the masculine term was important since normally only sons could inherit the father's wealth. Verse 17 makes very clear that the inheritance is part of the package—we are "heirs of God and joint heirs with Christ."

It would be wonderful if we could discover just how the earliest Christians used the term *Abba* in their prayers, in their corporate worship or in their everyday conversation. *Abba* was the intimate term used by first-century Jews to speak with their fathers. How thrilling it must have been for people who had been separated from God, by religious ritual and courses of priests in both Judaism and paganism, to be able to begin a conversation with God by calling God *Abba,* a term that went back to the earliest disciples, perhaps even to Jesus himself!

Paul ends this paragraph with a reference to suffering and glorification with Christ. This both sums up what it means to be a child of God and prepares the reader for the next section, which focuses on the coming glory.

A preacher could develop a sermon on each paragraph in this section, but since I prefer to preach on longer texts, the sample sermon that follows is based on all seventeen verses.

Paul's development forms a good structure for a sermon, as he takes us from God's act of redemption in Christ, through the power of the Holy Spirit in operation in the believer's life, to the status of children of God, including the expectation of the inheritance of glory. The sermon is rather didactic, which is not a bad thing in an age when we cannot assume much knowledge of the Bible among the people to whom we preach. The sermon can be personalized by the use of personal illustrations.

SERMON

The Work of the Trinity
(Romans 8:1–17)

Introduction

Isn't it wonderful to see the sunshine after several days of cloudy weather? That's how Romans 8 strikes me after reading Romans 7. In the earlier chapter, we have the cloudy weather of a person trying to serve God on human power alone. The frustrating experience leads to the cry, "Wretched man that I am! Who will rescue me?" And then we turn to the sunshine of "There is therefore now no condemnation for those who are in Christ Jesus." Even though we have a hint of the old clouds, in chapter 8 we bask in the sunshine, feeling its warmth and restoring power.

Sunshine encourages us; it empowers us; it warms us. That's what these verses do, too. They encourage; they empower; they warm. Better yet, through them, God's salvation encourages us; God's Spirit empowers us; and God's adoption warms us.

1. God's Salvation Encourages Us

Many of us, even many Christians, go through life carrying a heavy burden of guilt. We know all too well what Paul means when he says:

> I do not understand my own actions. For I do not do what I want, but I do the very thing I hate. Now if I do

what I do not want, I agree that the law is good. But in fact it is no longer I that do it, but sin that dwells within me. For I know that nothing good dwells within me, that is, in my flesh. I can will what is right, but I cannot do it. For I do not do the good I want, but the evil I do not want is what I do. (Rom. 7:15–19)

1. Experiencing such spiritual failure time and again, we learn to live with the guilt of failing to live up to God's expectations for us. We need to learn something from the apostle Paul here. As he confesses in other texts, no one was a greater sinner than he was. He had been a persecutor of Christians, endangering their lives and blaspheming their Lord. How did he learn to cope with such guilt?

2. He knew the good news that when we were still sinners Christ died for us. Even in the composition of the letter to the Romans, Paul deals with sin in general first and justification in general second. He deals with the personal feelings of guilt about sin only after he has assured people that Christ has overcome sin for us and that therefore we can become new creatures.

3. Then he dictates chapter 7, where he describes so vividly our failure to do what we know we should, followed by chapter 8, which begins, "There is therefore now no condemnation for those who are in Christ Jesus."

4. He could almost be paraphrasing the opening words of Isaiah 40:

Comfort, O comfort my people, says your God.
Speak tenderly to Jerusalem,
    and cry to her
that she has served her term,
    that her penalty is paid,
that she has received from the LORD's hand
    double for all her sins.

5. We need not carry that guilt any farther. We need not labor under the weight of that sin any more. Christ has lifted the burden. He has thrown it away. The penalty has been paid; the guilt is gone. "There is therefore now no condemnation for those who are in Christ Jesus." What a comfort!

2. God's Spirit Empowers Us

Verses 9–11 of our text are full of references to the Holy Spirit. Scholars like to argue about the details, but one thing is clear. Paul tells us that the Holy Spirit is given to us to swing the weight of our lives from the frustration and guilt of sin to the victory over sin made possible by the presence and power of the Holy Spirit.

The Spirit is not an option—an add-on—for the Christian life. The choice, Paul says, is between being in the flesh and being in the Spirit. In other words, to be a Christian is to live in the force field of God's Spirit.

Do not get mired down in terminology about the Spirit. Paul uses several different ways of naming the Spirit: Spirit of God, Spirit of Christ, Christ in you, the Spirit of him who raised Jesus from the dead, the one who raised Christ from the dead, and just plain Spirit. What we are dealing with here is the presence of God in power in our lives, no matter what terms we use to name that powerful presence.

The presence of the Spirit means the difference between death and life, between hostility to God and serving God. The reality of the Spirit is God's means of encouraging us believers during the difficulties of our lives.

The presence of the Spirit means that we have the ability to change. In Paul's words, we can "put to death the deeds of the body" (v. 13). This means that we can do, with the help of the Spirit, what we could not accomplish on our own, as Paul described it in chapter 7.

The presence of the Spirit means we can live in the assurance that we are not slaves to sin. Instead, we are children of God. The greatest encouragement of all is to know we belong, to know that we are part of a family, God's family.

3. God's Adoption Warms Us

To know we have that family relationship is tremendously pleasant. Those of us who were reared in a strong family know the feeling of leaving the house with the knowledge we are loved and the feeling of warmth when we return home.

Those who have not had that strong family relationship know they missed something important.

Paul tells us we can have that same warmth raised to the ultimate level. We can know that God loves us so much that God chose us—God adopted us into a family of which we are not worthy.

You can see some of the other adopted children in God's family. They are sitting around you this morning. It is obvious that none of us is worthy, but we have been chosen.

The ultimate warming factor is to know that our being in God's family means that we are "joint heirs with Christ." Christ became one of us so that we could become one like him. We live in the expectation of the glory of God's presence for eternity. That realization should warm our every cold mood.

Conclusion

Return to your homes, your work, your education, your own families. Return with the courage, the power, and the warmth of the knowledge that God in all aspects of divinity is at work with you, around you, among you, and within you to accomplish what is possible only through the work of the Trinity.

CHAPTER 13

Preaching from Romans
8:18–39

As we saw in the last chapter, Paul in Romans 8 proclaims the word of assurance to the Roman Christians and to us. Beginning with verse 18 he states some of his mind-boggling thoughts, this time relating the experience of justification of the individual human being with the restoration of the whole creation to its intended state.

So much is packed into these verses that the preacher has trouble deciding where to focus. Paul begins with reference to the whole creation—a theme that resonates with many Christians today because of our concern for the environment. He links that with hope, without which life is rather dismal. He links it with the frustration we feel from time to time, not knowing even how to pray.

Verses 28–30 frighten most of us, dealing as they do with the sovereignty of God and those theological terms: foreknowledge, predestination, calling, justification, and glorification. A sermon that attempts to define such terms would be a challenge to prepare and to hear. Then, in verses 31–39, Paul brings this section of the letter to a crashing climax with one of the most ringing declarations of hope and security in the scriptures. The section can be divided into two parts, each of which begins with a question: verse 31, "If God is for us, who is against us?" and verse 35, "Who will separate us from the love of Christ?"

I want to concentrate on verses 31–34. This passage often gets lost in the beauty of the verses following, but it presents the preacher with an unusual opportunity: a narrative format in the middle of a logical presentation. The opening question, "If God is for us, who is against us?" is answered with the brief summary of the story of the death of Christ for our sins: God "Who did not withhold his own Son, but gave him up for us, will he not with him also give us everything else?" The preacher can fill in the blanks of the events of the gospel and the application of it in the promise of "everything else."

This is followed by a subsidiary question, reply, and following question, "Who will bring any charge against God's elect? It is God who justifies. Who is to condemn?" In previous chapters, I have explained the justification God has made available through the faithfulness of Jesus Christ. If a sermon on this passage follows sermons on other parts of Romans, little exposition will be necessary here. However, if this is a free-standing sermon, the preacher will want to explain or illustrate justification by grace before proceeding.

Since chapter 8 starts with the proclamation, "There is therefore no condemnation for those who are in Christ Jesus," Paul's question, "Who is to condemn," was rhetorical. It sets up the narrative flow of the following sentence. Notice the order of these statements. We often read through verse 34 so quickly that we miss the effect of the order.

One possible affirmative reply to the question about condemnation is "Christ Jesus." We know (at least we think we do) this is absurd, but many people think of God as a heavenly policeman and Christ as God's deputy. So examine the sentence. "Christ Jesus, who died..." Since the death of Jesus was not for the wages of his own sin—he died because of our sin—he has a reason to condemn us. "Christ Jesus, who died, yes, who was raised...." A dead person's condemnation cannot harm us, but one raised from the dead has not only a reason but also the ability to condemn us. "Christ Jesus, who died, yes, who was raised, who is at the right hand of God...." He has the reason, the ability and the authority to condemn us since he is seated in the place of ultimate authority, God's right hand. "Christ Jesus, who died, yes who was raised, who is at the right hand of God, who indeed intercedes for us." Here is the good news, appreciated only when we slow down and let each clause sink in. The one who has a reason, the ability, and the authority to condemn us—the one who could be the prosecuting attorney in our eternal judgment trial—is instead our defense attorney. The only one who could condemn us is interceding for us. We receive great comfort, security, and hope in the realization that even when we condemn ourselves, Christ is doing the opposite. Christ is speaking our name in love to the God in whose hands rests our eternity, the one he and we can address as *Abba.*

The rest of the chapter is one illustration after another of what Christians need not fear—"Who will separate us from the love of Christ?" (8:35). The kind of love that drove the Son of God to die and live for those responsible for his death is not going to let anybody or anything come between the lover and the beloved. Not even "hardship, or distress, or persecution, or famine, or nakedness, or peril, or sword" can separate us from that love. It should be obvious that we can choose to live a life contrary to that love, but we can never make God stop loving us.

Verse 36 quotes Psalm 44:22 to describe how Paul saw the Christian life: daily slaughter. This is an unpleasant thought, but we can read about the slaughter of Christians in the first few centuries of the church's history and marvel at the confidence with which those believers faced pain and death. Paul claims that none of that was enough to convince him that God did not love him. If God loved him, who or what could ultimately hurt him? "No, in all these things we are more than conquerors through him who loved us" (8:37).

In verses 38 and 39 Paul brings the whole line of thought to a climax by challenging all the mysteries of creation. He has established that human powers cannot ultimately triumph over God's beloved. Here he examines all the extraterrestrial powers, real or imaginary, that caused fear among his contemporaries. "For I am convinced that neither death, nor life [over which we have no control even with all the discoveries of modern science], nor angels, nor rulers [those demons that are out of our control], nor things present, nor things to come [since time is the context in which we live and not our own contrivance], nor powers [by which he must mean those spiritual powers that will be destroyed in the end-time], nor height, nor depth [by which he is likely referring to terms of astrology], nor anything else in all creation will be able to separate us from the love of God in Christ Jesus our Lord."

It is hard to imagine how Paul could have listed any more terms that would have struck such fear into the hearts of people of his day. Each age of history seems to develop its own phobias, as has ours; but we can live in the assurance that the love of God is unconquerable. Nothing we or anybody else can do can make God stop loving us. In fact, because of that love, we can be assured that all things, even the bad things, are ultimately working together for good. Thank God.

This chapter gives us plenty of grist for the preaching mill. I have chosen to present a sermon on verses 31–34, an overlooked part of the chapter. I base it on my "slow reading" exegesis of those verses, following the narrative flow of Paul's statements to emphasize the astounding grace of God in Christ.

SERMON

"In That Case"
(Romans 8:31–34)

Introduction

The blame game is familiar to us. We see and hear a lot of condemnation going on. We blame our parents for the mess we have made of our lives. We blame the auto industry for the gas-guzzlers that pollute the air and fill the highways. We blame the rich people who work on Wall Street for the present economic problems. We blame the politicians for the tension in the world. We blame our bosses, our fellow workers, our neighbors, our spouses, our children. We can find somebody to blame for nearly every problem we face. Sometimes we even blame ourselves.

Our text for today indicates that the apostle Paul understood the blame game only too well. He had been on both sides of the game. He had blamed the woes of Israel on the Christians. Now as a Christian, he found others blaming him. Of one thing he was sure—God is not in the blame game. Oh, he could talk about God as the judge of all humanity, but when it came down to the verdict he was sure no condemnation was in store for Christ's followers.

How could he be so sure? We would all like such blessed assurance. Well, here is his explanation based on what he has already established—that "all have sinned." We have no right to condemn one another since we are all in the same condition before God. Only God can condemn justly, and God has given Jesus Christ, the Son of God, for us. That proves that God is for us, not against us. That leaves only one possibility:

1. "Christ Jesus." The sinless one is the only one who has the right to condemn. The sinless one is the only one who can condemn justly. You and I have no right to condemn others since we are sinners just as they are. The answer Jesus gave to those who brought to him a woman caught in the act of adultery applies in many situations in our lives: The one who is without sin may cast the first stone. Jesus has the right to condemn us.

2. "Christ Jesus, who died." The one who died because of our sins has a good reason to condemn us. Death, Paul said, is the wages of sin. The corollary would be that the one without sin does not deserve to die. But Jesus died. Paul said Jesus did it for our sins. The apostle has reminded us that humanly speaking a person would find it difficult to die even for a righteous person, if one existed. But Paul stated "while we were still sinners Christ died for us" (Rom. 5:8). That is not an even trade. Christ had a reason to condemn us.

3. "Christ Jesus, who died, yes, who was raised." Only a living person can condemn somebody, so Christ has the ability to condemn us. He is alive. We sometimes forget that. We remember at Christmas time that he was born. We remember on Good Friday that he died. We sing on Easter about his resurrection. During the rest of the year, we tend to forget that he is alive 24/7/365. Christ has the ability to condemn us.

4. "Christ Jesus, who died, yes, who was raised, who is at the right hand of God." In the minds of Paul and those to whom he was writing, to sit at the right hand of the ruler was to have power nearly equal to that of the ruler. Christ has the authority to condemn. He could issue the edict of condemnation from his position of divine authority. We are told that he will come again to judge the living and the dead. Christ has the right to condemn. Christ has the reason to condemn. Christ has the ability to condemn. Christ has the authority to condemn. That provides a logical answer to Paul's question, "Who is to condemn?"

5. "Christ Jesus, who died, yes, who was raised, who is at the right hand of God, who indeed intercedes for us." This last clause contains all the good news we ever need. Christ intercedes for us. He is the one who could condemn. He is the one who could be the prosecuting attorney in our case before the divine Judge. And what does Paul describe him as doing? What is Christ's role in this court case? He is acting as our defense attorney!

Conclusion

Our case is finished before it begins. The only one who can bring an accusation or present damaging evidence is our defense attorney, who is mediating on our behalf with the Judge. The judgment is "Righteous." The prisoner is set free. Let's celebrate.

CHAPTER 14

Preaching from Romans
10:1–21[1]

Romans 10 is part of one of the most fascinating sections of the New Testament. Chapters 9, 10, and 11 all deal with what appears to have been the primary problem of Paul's ministry—a biblical, theological, and personal problem. The problem is this: Why have God's chosen people rejected God's Messiah? Paul, a former persecutor of Christians, knew all too well the reality of this rejection. As a Christian who had studied his scriptures through the lens of the resurrection of Jesus, he now appeared to wonder how the Jews could have missed their own scriptural witness to this Messiah.

Chapter 9 expresses Paul's deep concern for his people and points out the course of God's election that led to the present situation where God has opened the gates of justification to the Gentiles on the basis of faith. In chapter 11, Paul declares that, in spite of all appearances, God has not rejected the people of God. In fact, God is accomplishing the justification of the Gentiles by means of the stumbling of the Israelites. Paul then warns the Gentiles not to get proud of the state of affairs, since God can also cut their branches out of the olive tree. The whole situation is a mystery, but Paul assures his readers that eventually "all Israel will be saved" (11:26). The section closes with a beautiful doxology.

Between these two chapters lies our text. It includes several well-known statements: "Christ is the end of the law" (v. 4), "if you confess with your lips that Jesus is Lord and believe in your heart that God raised him from the dead, you will be saved" (v. 9), and "faith comes from what is heard, and what is heard comes through the word of Christ" (v. 17). Any of these could become the basis of a sermon. If a preacher studies the whole context carefully, those sermons can be important expositions of scripture.

Another preaching approach from chapter 10 or from the whole three-chapter section is a study of how the early church used its Bible. Paul's quotations from and allusions to the Hebrew Scriptures in this section offer the preacher a case study in early Christian interpretation of scripture. Let's look more closely at the texts he refers to in chapter 10.

In verse 5, Paul names Moses and steps immediately into Deuteronomy 30. His stepping stone is a quotation from Leviticus 18:5, "the person who does these things will live by them." He has already dealt with this approach to the *Torah* beginning in 2:13, so here he does not have to argue his point that nobody actually obeys the law well enough to be justified by it. Furthermore, he has just stated (v. 4) that Christ is what the law was aiming for in the first place. He next contrasts the Leviticus statement with an interpretation of part of the final address of Moses to the Israelites. Before considering the words, think about the situations. Moses, the one who led the Israelites out of Egyptian bondage and through forty years in the wilderness, was giving the people his final instructions and motivations. The Israelites of Paul's day had no more authoritative words, the equivalent of the deathbed statement of the nation's founder.

Paul does not situate himself here as an interpreter explaining the meaning of Moses' words. Instead, he puts himself into the scene itself by making "the righteousness that comes from faith" the speaker of the words. For those who understood Leviticus as the words of Moses, it must have come as a shock to hear Paul using words of Moses to contradict words of Moses. The statements from Deuteronomy 30:12–14

are then interrupted by interpretive statements, much as the
Dead Sea scrolls show us. The interpretive method is called
pesher, which is a way to connect an ancient text with a
contemporary event or understanding.

So our translations use parentheses to enclose Paul's *pesher*
statements (vv. 6–8):

> "Do not say in your heart, 'Who will ascend into
> heaven?'" (that is, to bring Christ down) "or 'Who will
> descend into the abyss?'" (that is, to bring Christ up
> from the dead). But what does it say?
> > "The word is near you,
> >   on your lips and in your heart"
> (that is, the word of faith that we proclaim)

A quick comparison of this with the Hebrew text indicates
some major differences, but we must keep in mind that Paul
nearly always quoted from the Septuagint. Paul follows that
text here quite accurately. Note how easily Paul jumps from
Moses, the redeemer of Israel, to Jesus, the redeemer of all the
faithful. Any attempt to win salvation by one's own effort, either
by storming heaven or the abyss, is nonsense, since Christ has
already come from heaven and has already been raised from
the dead. The important part of Moses' statement is that the
word is near, and this Paul identifies with "the word of faith
that we proclaim." He introduces the argument of Romans with
the claim, "the gospel...is the power of God for salvation" (2:16).
This word of faith is available to all, free for the hearing.

Paul unpacks the reality of this word and its power to evoke
faith in verses 10–12, ending with the quotation from Joel 2:32,
"Everyone who calls on the name of the Lord shall be saved."
He proceeds to discuss the process of proclamation, ending
with a quotation from Isaiah 52:7, "How beautiful are the feet
of those who bring good news."

He then (v. 16) returns to the fact that not all have obeyed
this good news. He reminds people that this is nothing new.
Isaiah also cried out, "LORD, who has believed our message?"
(Isa. 53:1, author's translation) The Septuagint uses here the
Greek word *akoe,* which translates a Hebrew term related to

shema`*, which means "hear." The *shema` in Deuteronomy 6:4 was and continues to be the basic confession of faith and call to worship of Israel, so we are dealing with an issue of primary importance here. The NRSV translates the Isaiah text, "Who has believed what we have heard?" I do not understand why the translators failed to use the same translation here in Romans 10:16, since *akoe* carries the implication of hearing. The Hebrew Bible and the Christian Scriptures are clear that the message human beings proclaim they must first hear as a word of God from God.

Verse 17 brings all this together in a christological climax: "So faith comes from what is heard, and what is heard comes through the word of Christ." This verse has been translated and paraphrased in many different ways. The wording in the NRSV is as good as they come. The reading isliterally, "So faith comes out of hearing." Paul has consistently shown that the gospel or the *kerygma* elicits faith. Faith results in salvation. It is not just the process of hearing that produces faith in some magical sense. The hearing of the specific message of God—the kind of hearing called for in the ancient *shema`*—produces faith. This ready-to-obey hearing of the power of God for salvation results in faith/faithfulness. When that happens, the very expression of Christ himself is at work.

I come upon this latter idea because of Paul's choice of words in the second half of the verse: "*he de akoe dia rhematos Christou.*" This is literally, "but hearing by means of a word of Christ." The agency that produces faith is not human communication. The only agency that produces faith is the agency of divine speaking. Paul could have used the word *logos* here, but he chose the more concrete term *rhema*. *Logos* can refer to a message or a word as a whole text, but *rhema* normally refers to the act of pronouncing a specific set of syllables. This "word of Christ" must be more than just a message about Christ; it must refer to Christ himself speaking in the process of the human preaching of the gospel.

The sermon that follows grows out of this exegesis. It focuses on the place of words—especially spoken words—in our Christian lives. The order of the sections moves toward an evangelistic appeal. The sections could be put in other orders to lead to a commitment to bear verbal witness or even to encourage more preaching of the gospel. In any case, the place of speech is in the forefront.

SERMON ▰▰▰▰▰▰▰▰▰▰▰▰▰▰▰▰▰▰▰▰▰▰▰▰▰

Saving Words
(Romans 10:5–15)

Introduction

Our text from Romans 10 contains the most important words a human being can experience. They are saving words– words that speak about God's work of salvation for the human race, words by which we may respond to God's faithfulness, words by which God promises to respond to our faith.

For this reason, the text's author, the apostle Paul, imbedded his words in a speech of the greatest hero, leader, teacher, and prophet of his people: Moses. Paul did not just choose Moses as a vehicle for his saving words; he chose the words Moses spoke to the people of Israel the last time they would see him. This is the deathbed statement of Moses, so to speak. Deuteronomy 29 describes the scene. Moses summoned the people and gave them their final instructions, preparing them to move into the promised land.

All Israel held these words of Moses in great respect. Paul used them to frame some of his most important words to his fellow Christians. Paul tells about the saving words we preach, hear, and confess, as well as the saving words we can expect to hear from our Lord.

We Preach Saving Words

For most of us, our Christian faith started when we heard somebody speak about Jesus. A few people are converted by reading. That indicates that writing is also an evangelistic activity. For most of us, the words we *heard* turned us toward Christ. Knowing this, it seems strange that we tend to be so quiet about our faith in Christ Jesus. We tend to leave the preaching to the professionals—to the preachers who rarely meet the people who need to hear the saving words. The church has become a community of specialists though the world needs to see the consistency of a community of generalists. The world desperately needs a community of people all of whom are ready to bring the world the good news of salvation in Jesus Christ.

The saving words we preach need not be fancy words; they only need to be clear. They need not be technical; they only need to be understood. They need not be beautiful; they only need to speak to the hearts of people. When people hear and understand words in plain, brown wrappers about the death and resurrection of Jesus for human sin, they will recognize them as saving words from God.

We Hear Saving Words

Later in Romans 10 Paul said, "faith comes by hearing." When we hear words about the grace of God in Christ and the claims of that gracious Lord on our lives—when we hear such words and are ready to act on them—we come to faith. That step might be our first step in the direction of heaven, or it could be another in a long line of steps in that direction. Wherever we are in the journey Godward, "faith comes by hearing."

Each time we respond positively to saving words, our faith grows another notch. We can hear those words in many ways. They come to us in sermons and lessons in church, certainly, but they come also in the hymns and choruses we sing, in prayers, in our participation in the Lord's Supper, as well as in our private times of Bible reading and prayer. They surprise us sometimes in casual conversations and walks in the woods. In short, saving words are all around us. We can hear them if we pay attention—if we "listen up."

We Confess Saving Words

When we hear saving words, it is our time to confess them to others. Does it seem that I am talking in circles here? Well, I am. People speak saving words so that other people hear them, so that they, too, can speak them to yet others. Conversation is like that, you know. Lively conversations rarely proceed in an orderly fashion from start to finish. They more likely go round and round, one person's statement stimulating another's response.

The saving words of the good news about Jesus should proceed in the same way—like a normal conversation. We hear, respond, speak, listen, hear, respond, and speak again. Faith grows in such exchanges, and lives are changed. In other words, salvation happens.

God Speaks Saving Words

The mystery about saving words is how God gets involved in the process. Here is where understanding stops and faith takes over. In some mysterious way, when we human beings use our all-too-human language to speak saving words, God steps in and speaks the critical words: righteousness and salvation. Verse 10 of our text reads, "For one believes with the heart and so is justified, and one confesses with the mouth and so is saved." When Paul says a person is justified, he means that God graces that person with divine righteousness—a goodness we cannot attain or earn on our own. When Paul says a person is saved, he means that God marks that person to spend eternity in God's own presence. The final word is always God's word. For us who have come to faith in Christ, God promises that the final word will be a saving word, for as the prophet Joel put it, "Everyone who calls on the name of the Lord shall be saved."

CHAPTER 15

Preaching from Romans 12:1-2[1]

As is true in most of the letters of the apostle Paul, the first section deals with what it means to become and be a Christian and the later chapters deal with how one is to live as a Christian. Cranfield[2] suggests (as noted in chapter 1) that Paul's outline of the epistle comes from the foundational text, Habakkuk 2:4. Paul quoted this in Romans 1:17, "The one who is righteous will live by faith." Being righteous by faith is the concern of the first 11 chapters, and living by faith the concern of chapters 12–16. This is a strong possibility since the "by faith" term is in the middle of the sentence in the original.

Romans 12:1–2 stands at the beginning of the section on Christian living, while referring the reader back to what Paul had dealt with. This double face is signaled by the first two words in the Greek text, *parakalo oun,* translated "I appeal therefore." Paul appeals for action, but always with the gospel of justification by faith/faithfulness as his primary reference point. He paraphrases that reference point here with the words "by the mercies of God." Since Paul has used "mercy" in chapters 9 to 11 in place of "grace," he continues that usage here to refer to his whole development of the justification of us sinners by God through the faithful death and miraculous resurrection of Jesus Christ.

He appeals for what we usually refer to as living sacrifice. He prepared for this appeal in 6:13 by urging Christians, "No longer present your members to sin as instruments [or weapons] of wickedness, but present yourselves to God as instruments of righteousness." He uses the same verb in 12: "present your bodies as a...sacrifice." He bases the appeal in chapter 6 on what happened to them in their baptism. In chapter 12, the appeal looks to the whole picture of God's mercy as its foundation. In both cases, what he asks for is total commitment. In chapter 6, we are to present ourselves (*heautous*) to God. Here, it is our bodies (*somata*). There is no mistaking Paul's appeal here as applying to anything but the whole person. The danger in this sort of appeal is that people hear it as a spiritual demand that may or may not include all aspects of life; but when we include the body, there is no escaping the holistic outlook.

Sacrifices were, of course, well known in first-century Rome and elsewhere. The pagan religions, as well as the Jewish religion, practiced the sacrificing of animals and other produce of the land. The implication is that we owe our very lives to God, making them the appropriate gift for us to offer. Paul follows this in the original with three adjectives that describe the nature and purity of this sacrifice: living, holy, and acceptable to God. The first descriptor is "living." We are led to understand we are not expected to die for God though that was often the result of such sacrifice. No, in this case, we are to live for God. Everyday activity becomes a sacrifice to God. The second descriptor is "holy." Since Paul convinced us that "all have sinned," we might wonder how the presentation of our sinful bodies could be considered holy. However, the God who justifies is the God who gives life to the dead and creates from nothing. Therefore, we become holy not because of our innate goodness or by our good actions or intents. We are made holy by the Creator-Justifier. This explains how our sacrifice could be considered "acceptable to God." God has created us and then re-created us "to be conformed to the image of his Son" (8:29). So even in our shift to living the Christian life, we are thrown back on the mercies of God to make us holy and acceptable sacrifices.

The last part of verse 1 may seem strange. Paul says, this act of sacrifice is *ten logiken latreian humon.* The *logiken latreian* is a challenge to translate. "Your spiritual worship" is a reasonable translation, but it indicates the difficulty of rendering in English both the ambiguity of the Greek terms and the Greek word order. The first term looks like a relative of our English word *logic,* which it is. Our penchant to neatly categorize and overanalyze ideas and human experiences causes us to try to decide here between "spiritual" and "logical." Paul likely had both of those characteristics in mind with the use of this term since philosophers in his day dealt not just with what we label the rational, but also with what we label the spiritual.

The second of Paul's terms can mean either "service" in general or "service of worship." We might argue that Paul would have had difficulty seeing the distinction between service of God and worship of God. Our use in English (as well as German) of "service" in relation to worship rituals carries that ambiguity nicely. When we serve, we worship; when we worship, we serve. If that is not so, then something is basically wrong with our sacrifice.

The final word in the sentence, however, is the most puzzling. Why would Paul end this sentence with the second person plural possessive pronoun? We cannot elegantly translate it in this order: the logical/spiritual service of worship *of you* [all]. But such word order is not at all strange in Greek. Greek often uses such word order to indicate emphasis. Is Paul doing this to emphasize "your"? Why would he do that? Think about his situation and that of the Roman Christians.

Paul was in Corinth; they were in Rome. These two major cities of the Roman Empire were filled with what he might categorize as "spiritual worship." They had more than their share of pagan temples, mystery religion cults, Jewish synagogues, and schools of philosophy. Nearly anywhere these believers looked, they could see places dedicated to spiritual or rational services. So Paul is likely pointing out to them the contrast to the peculiarly Christian service of worship. At those other places, people gave of their wealth (including animals and crops), of their emotions (in the mystical mystery religions), or of their minds (in the schools of philosophy). The peculiarly

Christian act, however, includes all of that and more; it is a total self-sacrifice, even of the body.

Verse 2 fills out the picture of this sacrifice. To be a living sacrifice means that the age we live in is no longer our standard or our primary influence. We are being renewed, re-created, reborn every moment of our lives. The negative side of Paul's statement does not use the normal term for world (*kosmos*). Instead, Paul uses the Greek words *to aioni touto,* "this age or aeon." Every age in human history has offered models for human actions and relationships. Paul insists that none of them is an appropriate model for Christians to conform their lives to.

One could speculate about the various possibilities for such influence in Paul's aeon. Even the Mosaic law would fit here. Paul has already shown that even this teaching that comes from God's own self-revelation is inadequate to justify us before God or to guide our lives. This is true not because it is weak, but because we are (Rom. 8:3). The only way we can live the life of sacrifice is through constant renewal. Such renewal is possible only by the work of God's Spirit in and among us. The Spirit can renew our minds, minds darkened and hardened by sin (1:21). This is the only true metamorphosis (Greek *metamorphousthe,* "transformed").

Living sacrifice by means of renewal by the Spirit is the only way to discern God's will. The verb *dokimazein,* translated in the NRSV and other versions as "discern" can mean also "test" and "approve." In other words, we can be walking testimonials of God's will. Our lives can show we understand that will and can demonstrate the kind of life God approves of. We can be God's documentation. Just as in verse 1 Paul used three adjectives to describe the appropriate sacrifice, here in verse 2 he ends with three adjectives to define what he means by the will of God: *to agathon kai euareston kai teleion.* The good, the acceptable, and the perfect are high on the scale of virtues on anybody's list. Standing alone, they sound rather abstract; linked with the material that follows, they become concrete. How we treat one another in the body of believers, how we deal with people in our communities, how we relate to our governments, how we show the love of Christ to our neighbors, and how we become reconciled with those we have offended or been offended by are daily human experiences and attitudes. Each of these is connected with our being living sacrifices through the renewal of our minds.

There is no neat division here into categories, such as social ethic, business ethic, personal morals, and so on. This appeal is all encompassing. The self-sacrifice does not stop halfway. It is all or nothing. Only the sacrifice of all is good, acceptable, and perfect. This is a big order, but Paul rooted it in the mercies of God, with whom all things are possible.

The sermon that follows attempts to lead the hearer to understand that salvation is more than accepting the gracious forgiveness of our sins. Salvation means that we are to live in a way that reflects the reality of the grace of God in our lives.

SERMON ▪

Saving Life
(Romans 12:1-2)

Introduction

The eleven chapters that precede our Romans text describe from many angles the saving grace of God. God's mercy, as the psalmist says, "shall follow me all the days of my life" (Ps. 23:6). Paul has shown God's mercy in ancient history and in Jesus and the church. He has shown God's mercy to the Jew and also to the Greek. He has shown God's mercy to the sinner as well as the righteous. He has proclaimed God's mercy to the hopeless, to the helpless, even to those who did not know they needed it. He has quoted God's statement to Moses (Ex. 33:19), "I will have mercy on whom I have mercy, and I will have compassion on whom I have compassion" (9:15).

Now chapter 12 opens with an appeal—an exhortation—on the basis of the mercy of God. Not only does our eternal salvation depend on God's mercy, but the Christian life also grows out of that mercy. As we saw in an earlier sermon, God's grace remains active in the lives of people like us who have received it. So Paul exhorts us to live a life appropriate to our status as recipients of the mercy of God—that is, to live a saving life.

The Saving Life Is Offered to God

If everything we are and everything we have is a gift of God, then the most appropriate action we can take is to offer all of it back to God. That is precisely Paul's opening exhortation—"to present your bodies as a...sacrifice." This is, of course, a call not for suicide, but for consecration, as the rest of the verse shows. Paul described our sacrifice as "living, holy, and acceptable to God."

Frances Havergal's penned these familiar hymn words after a wonderful experience of God's mercy moving in the lives of people around her. Her poetic words spell out the life offered to God:

Take my life, and let it be consecrated, Lord, to Thee.
Take my moments and my days; let them flow in
    ceaseless praise.
Take my hands, and let them move at the impulse of
    thy love.
Take my feet, and let them be swift and beautiful for
    thee.

Take my voice, and let me sing always, only, for my
    King.
Take my lips, and let them be filled with messages
    from Thee.
Take my silver and my gold; not a mite would I
    withhold.
Take my intellect, and use every power as Thou shalt
    choose.

Take my will, and make it Thine; it shall be no longer
    mine.
Take my heart, it is Thine own; it shall be Thy royal
    throne.
Take my love, my Lord, I pour at Thy feet its
    treasure store.
Take myself, and I will be ever, only, all for Thee.

Have you ever made a list of aspects of your life that you have offered to God? Maybe you should do that. Is there a part you have guarded from the altar? Some of your moments or days, perhaps? Some things your hands do or some places your feet take you? Words that cross your lips? Money through your bank account? It is time for each of us to pray: "Take my love, my Lord, I pour at Thy feet its treasure store. Take myself, and I will be ever, only, all for Thee."

The Saving Life Is Formed by God

What determines the form of your life, that life you have offered to God? Can you evaluate the power of the various influences on your life? How about the influence of your family, or your education, or your status in the community? Where does the church fit in? The primary question, according to our text, is the origin of the formative influences. "Do not be conformed to this world" is the negative side of Paul's exhortation. The term Paul uses here for "world" is "aeon." Do not let this age—whatever its primary influences may be—force you into its mold. Oh, it tries hard enough and succeeds too often. We are surrounded by images and sounds that try to form us—pictures on billboards, on television, on our computer screens, in our newspapers and magazines—images trying to convince us to buy a product or a service. The sounds of music and speech come at us from all directions trying to form us in mind, body, and spirit. From the seemingly harmless ads for stuff to give us the best-looking lawn in the neighborhood to the invitations to immorality, this age of ours is trying to get us to conform to its standards.

But the primary influence for us as Christians should come from a source outside our era. We are to "be transformed by the renewing of [our] minds." Such renewal can happen only through God's Holy Spirit. This means that we are not left to our own willpower or to our own self-discipline to accomplish the saving life. God is ready and eager to work it out for us. Once again, it is a matter of turning life over to God. As we offer life to God, we invite the Holy Spirit to work in us to renew our lives beginning with our minds.

The Saving Life Is Oriented to God

When our minds are renewed, we have a new way to orient our lives. The mind of this age is oriented to the things, the stuff, of our world. That means we give most of our attention to the accumulation of stuff. The mind renewed by the Holy Spirit is oriented to the reality of God in the world. That means that things and services offered by our world play a secondary role in our lives. Our primary attention focuses on the eternal reality that is God.

This is what Paul means when he writes, "so that you may discern what is the will of God—what is good and acceptable and perfect." Most people are disgusted from time to time with the immorality or with the uncaring attitude of other people, but we rarely know what to do about it. In a world like ours it seems impossible even to know "what is good and acceptable and perfect," let alone be able to do it. Yet the Christian promise—the good news—is that God's work of renewal in our minds leads us to that discernment and way of life, because it leads us to focus our lives on the reality of God in the world.

The Saving Life Reflects God's Grace

That new focus results in a different kind of life—a life that reflects the grace of God. Paul exhorts us to live that life and does so "by the grace given to [him]." Toward the end of his exhortation, he points out that "[w]e have gifts that differ according to the grace given to us." We would do well to read the rest of chapter 12 and go on through chapters 13, 14, and 15 to see how Paul describes the life of the believer whose mind has been renewed by God's Spirit. In this description, we see humility and respect for others. We see eagerness to serve others. We see people who are peacemakers, people who overcome evil with good, people who obey the law, people who are tolerant of those whose opinions differ from theirs. In other words, here we see the people we would like to have living in our neighborhoods. They are the people our neighbors would like to have living near them.

Does your life show the grace of God to your neighbors or to the people you work with, study with, and play with? Does your life attract people to the saving grace of God? It is high time for each of us to let go of this age and let God lead us to be the people we really want to be. Lay your life on God's altar, and let God make the necessary alterations.

The Importance of Romans Today

Romans always entices and invites us to say more, but I must draw this volume to a close. I do so with a personal testimony. I go to the whole Bible expecting a word from God to help me and others as we live life in all its different circumstances. Because of my long and intimate acquaintance with Romans, I turn to it often. I cannot claim never to have been disappointed, but I must confess that those times when God's word has not spoken clearly to me have been when I was resistant to it. I return often to Romans 10:17 to remind myself that hearing is basic, that hearing is an act of the human will, and that I, therefore, must choose to hear God speaking.

I have lived and preached long enough to say with assurance that until a preacher hears—really hears—a word for himself or herself the preacher won't have a strong word for anybody else. I have long disliked the metaphor of a bridge for biblical preaching, because a bridge is so static, so stable, and so disconnected from the traffic it carries. No metaphor does justice to the preacher's process of internalizing a message from God and then communicating that message to people so they can actualize it in their daily lives.

The epistle to the Romans is a great example of that process. Paul's own personality shines through even in passages where he appears to be doing an objective description. In other places, he reveals himself quite clearly. The message of sin and justification, leading to total dedication and Christian living comes not just from Paul's analysis. Such personal words come even more from his experience. Paul's life experience was, of course, unique, just as is yours and mine. However, hearing this message filtered through Paul's life helps us to see its relevance to our lives.

This underscores the importance of our being as transparent as appropriate when we communicate God's word to God's people. Preaching never works when the preacher attempts to be objective. Nor does it help much when the preacher just "shares" her or his own experiences with the congregation. Rather, when the preacher lets the text touch vulnerable spots in his or her own life and then proclaims the message of God via that experience, the text will come alive for the people and more importantly, God will come across as a powerful and gracious reality.

What people need in an age of stress and skepticism is the awareness of God's presence. Preaching is a primary means to that end, and preaching from Romans is a great way to accomplish it.

> How beautiful upon the mountains
> > are the feet of the messenger
> > > who announces peace,
> > who brings good news,
> > > who announces salvation. (Isa. 52:7)

Preface

[1]"Preaching From Romans," in *Preaching Through Tears: Essays in Honor of Wayne E. Shaw,* ed. John D. Webb and Joseph C. Grana III (Lincoln, Ill.: Lincoln Christian College and Seminary Alumni Association, 2000), 137–55.

[2]*The New Revised Standard Version Bible;* Copyright © 1989, Division of Christian Education of the National Council of the Churches of Christ in the United States of America.

Introduction

[1]J. C. O'Neill, *Paul's Letter to the Romans* (Baltimore: Penguin Books, 1975).

[2]Mark D. Nanos, *The Mystery of Romans: The Jewish Context of Paul's Letter* (Minneapolis: Fortress Press, 1996).

[3]Alexander Campbell's "Sermon on the Law" was first published in *The Millennial Harbinger,* 3d series, vol. 3, no. 9, September 1846. A photo reprint of the sermon, with renumbered pages, was issued as a separate publication (*Sermon on the Law* by Alexander Campbell: Delivered at Cross Creek, Va., 1816) by Lincoln Christian College Press in 1971. The sermon, with an introduction by Charles Alexander Young, appears in *Historical Documents Advocating Christian Union,* ed. C. A. Young (Chicago: The Christian Century Press, 1904; rep., Joplin, Mo.: College Press, 1985), 211–82. An electronic version of the essay has been produced from the College Press reprint (1976) of *The Millennial Harbinger,* ed. Alexander Campbell (Bethany, Va.: A. Campbell, 1846), 493–521. It is available at http://www.mun.ca/rels/restmov/restmov.html.

[4]Phillip Melanchthon labeled it thus in both his *Loci Communes* (1520) and his commentary on Romans (1521).

[5]Gunther Bornkamm has called it Paul's theological testament. See *Geschichte und Glaube II* (München: Chr. Kaiser Verlag, 1971), 120–39.

[6]See *The Romans Debate,* ed. Karl P. Donfried (Minneapolis: Augsburg, 1977, rev. 2001).

[7]Augustine, *Confessions,* trans. Edward B. Pusey (New York: Pocket Library, 1957), the end of Book 8, 147–48.

[8]Cited in Roland Bainton, *Here I Stand* (New York: The New American Library of World Literature, 1950), 49–50.

[9]Cited in John Dillenberger, *Martin Luther* (Garden City: Doubleday & Co., 1961), 19.

[10]*The Journal of John Wesley* (Chicago: Moody Press, n.d.), 64.

[11]Karl Barth, *The Epistle to the Romans,* trans. Edwyn Hoskins (London: Oxford University Press, 1933, reprint 1975), 12.

[12]C. K. Barrett, *A Commentary on the Epistle to the Romans* (London: Adam & Charles Black, 1973), vi.

Chapter 1: What Romans Says about Preaching

[1] *Pesher* is a method of interpretation used broadly in the Dead Sea Scrolls. It is characterized by the phrase, "This is that which was written." It is seen several times in the New Testament, for instance, Acts 2:16.

[2] Several older manuscripts read "the word of God," but the best and oldest of the texts available read "Christ." This might indicate that early scribes recognized the high view of preaching being unfolded in this passage and inadvertently or intentionally shifted to the more familiar "word of God."

Chapter 2: What Romans Says about Creation

[1] Much of the material in this chapter is from my unpublished dissertation, "Creation in Romans," presented to the Protestant theological faculty of Eberhard Karls University, Tübingen, Germany, 1980.

[2] Gerhard Von Rad, *Weisheit in Israel* (Neukirchen: Neukirchener Verlag, 1970), 214. English: *Wisdom in Israel,* trans. James D. Martin (London: SCM Press, 1972), 164.

[3] William Sanday and Arthur Headlam, *The Epistle To The Romans,* The International Critical Commentary (Edinburgh: T. & T. Clark, 1895, 1977), 36.

[4] For a clear argument of this view, see C. E. B. Cranfield, *A Critical and Exegetical Commentary on the Epistle to the Romans,* The International Critical Commentary (Edinburgh: T. &. T. Clark, 1975), I, 156–57.

[5] Ulrich Wilckens, *Der Brief an die Römer,* vol. 1 (Zürich: Benziger Verlag, 1978), 133.

[6] Günther Bornkamm, "Gesetz und Natur," in *Studien zu Antike und Urchristentum: Gesammelte Aufsätze,* vol. 2 (Munich: Chr. Kaiser. 1959), 98.

[7] Bornkamm, "Gesetz und Natur," 101.

[8] Aristotle, *Nicomachaen Ethics,* 1128a, 31–32, speaks of the refined man as *nomos hon heauto*—quoted by Cranfield, 157, footnote 3.

[9] Otto Michel, *Der Brief an die Römer* (Göttingen: Vandenhoeck & Ruprecht, 1978), 119, thinks Paul is remembering Abraham as the model of Gentile righteousness.

[10] The wisdom tradition identified the Gentile ethical instinct with the *Torah.* Hartmut Gese has shown this connection in *Zur biblischen Theologie* (Munich: Chr. Kaiser, 1977), 68–78, where he claims (69): "es wäre in dieser theologischen Tradition undenkbar, daß es eine Welt und Schöpfungsordnung unabhängig von und neben dem Gesetz gäbe, vielmehr muß sich beides berühren, ja es sind verschiedene Stufen *einer* Offenbarung" (his emphasis): "it would have been unthinkable in this theological tradition that there was a world and a creative order independent from and parallel to the Law. It was much more the case that the two must touch one another; indeed, they are differing stages of the one revelation." George Howard makes a similar connection in *Paul: Crisis in Galatia* (Cambridge: Cambridge University Press, 1979), 74–82. He argues that the inescapable conclusion of Paul's understanding was to identify Judaism and paganism. Cf. also Stuhlmacher, "Das Gesetz als Thema biblischer Theologie," *Zeitschrift für Theologie und Kirche* 75 (1978): 256, 274–76.

[11] Helmut Koester, *nomos physeos:* "The Concept of Natural Law in Greek Thought," in *Religions in Antiquity,* ed. J. Neusner (Leiden: E. J. Brill, 1968),

522–30, argues that in Greek thought *nomos* and *physeos* were antitheses. Even the Stoics never used the term *nomos physeos*. What was translated into Latin as *lex naturae* was *logos physeos*. The general idea that a person is able to discern a structure in nature, and to live accordingly was a major Stoic theme. Paul's contemporary Philo did (see Koester, 530ff.) combine the terms and defined *nomos physeos* in terms of the *Torah*. Thus Paul, while never going as far as Philo in exegeting the Old Testament in terms of Greek philosophy, nevertheless interpreted the situation of the Gentiles with the help of Hellenistic concepts.

[12]Robert Jewett, *Paul's Anthropological Terms: A Study of their Use in Conflict Situations* (Leiden: E. J. Brill, 1971), 332.

[13]Wisdom of Solomon 17:11. Cf. also the survey by C. A. Pierce, *Conscience in the New Testament* (London: SCM Press, 1955), 54–59.

[14]Strack-Billerbeck, *Kommentar zum Neuen Testament aus Talmud und Midrash*, vol. 4, no. 1 (Munich: C. H. Beck'sche Verlagsbuchhandlung, 1974–75), 466.

[15]Bornkamm, *Gesetz und Natur*, 115–17. Pierce, *Conscience*, 54, defines conscience as "the pain suffered by man, and therefore as a creature involved in the order of things, when by his acts completed or initiated, he transgresses the moral limits of his nature."

[16]Philo, *de Decalogo*, trans. F. H. Colson, Loeb Classical Library, Philo vol. 7 (Cambridge, Mass. Harvard University Press, 1929–1962), 87, describes the activity of a conscience, but uses a different term: "For every soul has for its birth-fellow and house mate a monitor [*elegchos*] whose way is to admit nothing that calls for censure, whose nature is ever to hate evil and love virtue, who is its accuser and its judge in one."

[17]C. Maurer, *"sunoida ktl.,"* *Theological Dictionary of the New Testament*, ed. Gerhard Friedrichs, vol. 7 (Grand Rapids: Eerdmans, 1971), 917.

[18]Klaus Haacker, "Exegetische Probleme des Römerbriefes," *Novum Testamentum* 20: 6–9, however, suggests that *hemera* here need not be understood completely as the day of judgment but more generally as one of a number of instances when human thought plays the role of prosecutor or advocate.

[19]R. H. Charles, ed. *Apocrypha and Pseudepigrapha of the Old Testament*, vol. 2 (Oxford: The Clarendon Press, 1971, original 1913), 229.

[20]H. Gese, *Zur biblischen Theologie*, 68–78.

[21]Gustaf Aulen, *Christus Victor: An Historical Study of the Three Main Types of the Idea of Atonement*, trans. A. G. Hebert (New York: The Macmillan Co., 1960), 70.

[22]This is not to criticize the classic study of natural religion by William Temple, *Nature, Man and God, Being the Gifford Lectures of 1932–33 and 1933–34* (London: Macmillan and Co., 1934).

Chapter 3: What Romans Says about Sin

[1]Bob Dylan, "Gotta Serve Somebody," from *Slow Train Coming*, Columbia Records, 1979, copyright © 1979 Special Rider Music.

[2]*The Old Testament Pseudepigrapha*, ed. James H. Charlesworth, trans. M. D. Johnson, vol. 2 (Garden City, N.Y.: Doubleday, 1985), 281.

Chapter 4: What Romans Says About Justification/Righteousness

[1]For recent thought on the concept of grace, see the journal *Interpretation* 57/1 (January 2003), especially the articles by Jouette M. Bassler, "Grace: Probing the Limits," and Ellen T. Charry, "The Grace of God and the Law of Christ."

Chapter 5: What Romans Says about Eschatology

[1]Gerhard Kittel, *"doxa," Theological Dictionary of the New Testament* (TDNT), ed. Gerhard Kittel, trans. Geoffrey W. Bromiley, vol. 2 (Grand Rapids: W. B. Eerdmans, 1964), 237.

[2]C. John Collins, *"kbd," New International Dictionary of Old Testament Theology & Exegesis* (NICOTT), ed. Willem A. VanGemeren, vol. 2 (Grand Rapids: Zondervan, 1997), 577–87, sees "weight" as the central meaning of the Hebrew term. The noun meaning *honor* or *glory* may be associated with "dignity, wealth or high position; respect or reverence from others; or the object of respect."

[3]Kittel, TDNT, 245.

[4]Collins, NICOTT, 580, refers to the "external splendor" or what is "visibly expressed" of the dignity or honor of a person or object. Claus Westermann, *"kbd to be heavy," Theological Lexicon of the Old Testament,* ed. Ernst Jenni, Claus Westermann; trans. Mark E. Biddle (Peabody: Mass.: Hendrickson, 1997; German ed., 1971, 1976), II, 593, sees that "trees and woods or mountain forests also have *"kabod"* or wealth and respect.

[5]Collins, NICOTT, 581, calls *kabod* "a technical term for God's manifest presence." Schweizer, *pneuma,* TDNT, vol. 6, 417, footnote 551: *"doxa*...denotes the nature of God, but also of the angels." The *targum* on Isaiah 6:1–14 uses "glory of the Lord" as a substitute for the tetragrammaton.

[6]*Apocalypse of Moses (Life of Adam and Eve)* 20:2 and 21:6, *The Old Testament Pseudepigrapha,* ed. James H. Charlesworth, trans. M. D. Johnson, vol. 2 (Garden City, N.Y.: Doubleday, 1985), 281.,

[7]See also the *Genesis Rabbah: The Judaic Commentary to the Book of Genesis,* trans. Jacob Neusner (Atlanta: Scholars Press, 1985), on Gen. 12:6.

[8]1 Enoch 62:16 promises that the "righteous and elect...shall wear the garments of glory. These garments of yours shall become the garments of life from the Lord of the Spirits" (Charlesworth, *Old Testament Pseudepigrapha,* vol. 1, 44). This echoes the promise in Daniel 12:3: "Those who are wise will shine like the brightness of the heavens, and those who lead many to righteousness like the stars for ever and ever." Cf. also *Apocalypse of Moses,* 20ff.

[9]Rudolf Bultmann, *The Gospel of John,* trans. G. R. Beasley-Murray, R. W. N Hoare, and J. K. Riches (Philadelphia: The Westminster Press, 1971), 496.

Chapter 6: What Romans Says about Law/*Torah*

[1]It is unclear whether the beginning point of the fourteen years is Damascus or the visit to Jerusalem that he described in Galatians 1:18. If it were the latter, the total time was seventeen years.

Chapter 7: What Romans Says about Ethics

[1]Richard B. Hays, *The Moral Vision of the New Testament* (San Francisco: Harper SanFrancisco, 1996) treats this aspect of Paul's ethic. In a later chapter (379–406), he applies this line of thought to the issue of homosexuality.

[2]For a more complete exegesis of these verses, see chapter 15.

[3]Martin Luther, *Lectures on Romans,* ed. and trans. Wilhelm Pauck (Philadelphia: Westminster Press, 1961), says, "For being comes before doing, but being-acted-upon comes even before being," 321.

[4]Mark D. Nanos, *The Mystery of Romans: The Jewish Context of Paul's Letter* (Minneapolis: Fortress Press, 1996), 289–336.

[5]For an accessible rhetorical analysis of the passage see Philip H. Towner, "Romans 13:1–7 and Paul's Missiological Perspective," in *Romans and the People of God,* ed. Sven K. Soderlund and N. T. Wright (Grand Rapids: Eerdmans, 1999), 160–62.

Chapter 9: Preaching from Romans 1:18–3:26

[1]For an excellent summary of the issue and identical constructions elsewhere, especially in Galatians, see Richard B. Hays, *The Faith of Jesus Christ: The Narrative Substructure of Galatians 3:1–4:11* (Grand Rapids: William B. Eerdmans, 2001). For Romans 3, see 156–61.

[2]Karl A. Menninger, *Whatever Became of Sin?* (New York: Hawthorn Books, 1973).

[3]Leonard Bernstein, copyright © Boosey & Hawkes; used by permission.

Chapter 10: Preaching from Romans 4:1–25

[1]The first seventeen verses of this chapter are specified to be read on the second Sunday in Lent, year A. Verses 13–25 are listed as a lectionary reading for Proper 5, year A (or Ordinary 11, year A).

Chapter 11: Preaching from Romans 5:1–11

[1]The Revised Common Lectionary lists these verses to be read on Proper 6, year A (or Ordinary 10, year A).

[2]"Since Jesus Came into My Heart," words by Rufus Henry McDaniel, 1914.

[3]"Because He Lives," words by Gloria and William J. Gaither, copyright © Gaither Music, 1971.

[4]"What the World Needs Now Is Love," by Burt Bacharach and Hal David, copyright © Hal Leonard Corporation.

Chapter 12: Preaching from Romans 8:1–17

[1]The lectionaries divide this chapter differently. They call for 8:1–11 to be read on Lent 5A or Proper 10A/Ordinary 15A. They list verses 12–25 for Proper 11A/Ordinary 16A, Trinity B, and Pentecost C. This is overlapped by the choice of verses 22–27 for Pentecost B and verses 26–39 for Proper 12A/Ordinary 17A. Compared with the scarcity of earlier lectionary passages from Romans, it is obvious that chapter 8 is seen as important for the life of the church.

Chapter 14: Preaching from Romans 10:1–21

¹The lectionary committees have chosen Romans 10:5–15 to be read for Proper 14A/Ordinary 18A and for Lent 1C. To limit ourselves to these verses is to overlook the very personal statement by which Paul opens the chapter and the important statement about preaching and its roots in the Hebrew Scriptures by which Paul ends the chapter.

Chapter 15: Preaching from Romans 12:1–2

¹Romans 12:1–8 is listed in the lectionaries to be read on Proper 16A/Ordinary 21A. Since verses 3–8 deal with the nature and ministries of the church, including them is appropriate. However, I have chosen to concentrate on the first two verses, because they stand as an introduction to the rest of the epistle, just as 1:16–17 do for the early part.

²C. E. B. Cranfield, *Romans: The International Critical Commentary* (Edinburgh: T. & T. Clark, 1975, 1979).

Printed in the United States
22820LVS00002B/97-255

9 780827 229792